NEEDS ASSESSMENT

NEEDS ASSESSMENT
AN OVERVIEW

James W. Altschuld | **David Devraj Kumar**
The Ohio State University | *Florida Atlantic University*

Series Editor: James W. Altschuld

NEEDS ASSESSMENT KIT **1**

SAGE

Los Angeles | London | New Delhi
Singapore | Washington DC

For information:

SAGE Publications, Inc.
2455 Teller Road
Thousand Oaks,
  California 91320
E-mail: order@sagepub.com

SAGE Publications India Pvt. Ltd.
B 1/I 1 Mohan Cooperative
  Industrial Area
Mathura Road, New Delhi 110 044
India

SAGE Publications Ltd.
1 Oliver's Yard
55 City Road
London EC1Y 1SP
United Kingdom

SAGE Publications
  Asia-Pacific Pte. Ltd.
33 Pekin Street #02-01
Far East Square
Singapore 048763

Printed in the United States of America.

Library of Congress Cataloging-in-Publication Data

Altschuld, James W.
Needs assessment: an overview/James William Altschuld, David Devraj Kumar.
      p. cm.
Includes bibliographical references and index.
ISBN 978-1-4129-7584-1 (pbk.)
1. Strategic planning. 2. Needs assessment. I. Kumar, David D. II. Title.
HD30.28.A3885 2010
658.4'012—dc22

2009015173

This book is printed on acid-free paper.

09   10   11   12   13   10   9   8   7   6   5   4   3   2   1

Acquisitions Editor:	Vicki Knight
Associate Editor:	Sean Connelly
Editorial Assistant:	Lauren Habib
Production Editor:	Brittany Bauhaus
Copy Editor:	Melinda Masson
Typesetter:	C&M Digitals (P) Ltd.
Proofreader:	Victoria Reed-Castro
Indexer:	Diggs Publication Services, Inc.
Cover Designer:	Candice Harman
Marketing Manager:	Stephanie Adams

Brief Contents

Detailed Contents

Preface

For Jim Altschuld, this book and KIT are milestones in a journey that began 30 years ago when he came across what was a relatively new concept to him—needs assessment. He stumbled onto the work of Belle Ruth Witkin, who later became his guide and mentor on the topic, and in the process, a close and dear friendship was nourished. Now he is delighted to continue exploring the topic with David Kumar, another colleague and friend of long standing.

We sincerely hope that this effort enhances the theoretical and practical foundations laid by Witkin in her 1984 treatise on needs assessment. Two books followed (Altschuld & Witkin, 2000; Witkin & Altschuld, 1995) that expanded what was done before but did not go far enough in explaining how to do an assessment, in providing guidelines for the use of results, and so forth. The meaty details of needs assessment were treated somewhat superficially.

❖ POINT OF VIEW

How was this KIT designed? The goals are to provide specifications for the steps of Witkin and Altschuld's (1995) three-phase model of needs assessment and numerous hands-on procedures for implementing an assessment. This may appear simple to do, but in reality it is difficult. There are so many ways to conduct an investigation of needs that the KIT could get very long and expensive. That length could turn off those interested in needs assessment or individuals who perform assessments for their organizations. Therefore, we did the following:

- The assessment process is portrayed in sufficient depth to assist others in their own efforts while not attacking the endeavor from a prescribed, straitjacket viewpoint. Adopt, adapt, and tailor what is in the KIT for local contexts, politics, and resource constraints.

- Only the most used methods and procedures are covered.

- A lot of examples are discussed so that those doing assessments can see ways to make them work in quite diverse settings.

- Included are many tables, figures, and checklists that should be helpful to you.

❖ AUDIENCES FOR THIS BOOK AND THE KIT

Due to the applied emphasis, do not assume that the audience is only practitioners. The books in the KIT are a balance between practical strategies in concert with our best understanding of the literature and issues involved in needs assessments. This should fit implementers and those who study the process from a more academic basis. We also suggest that the KIT is a must for the bookshelf of practitioners including managers/decision makers, facilitators of an assessment, members of a needs assessment committee (NAC), and organizational staff. Decision makers benefit by gaining a sense of what a full and comprehensive effort entails without having to know all the nuances of every technique. They will appreciate what it takes to do an assessment, get a feel for some of its complexity, and lastly see how it relates to organizational change and learning. When leadership is aware of its potential, the endeavor should lead to growth and development.

The KIT would be a worthwhile addition to the library of the facilitator of an assessment effort. There are helpful hints for conducting NAC meetings; collating data; depicting results in a manner that leads to comprehension of what has gone on and its importance to the organization; communicating to others; documenting the work; and so forth. It also provides coverage of the subtle issues that impede doing a quality job. It enables even an experienced facilitator to anticipate the unexpected in needs assessment, and one will find innovative ways to implement procedures.

Members of the NAC will see the KIT as useful. It has not been written as a highly technical source that has value but doesn't focus enough on the working circumstances of the NAC. Committee members will learn from the KIT, but compared to the facilitator, they should skim some sections and concentrate on others for tasks with which they are involved. Lastly, having a copy of all of the books available for staff and personnel of the organization is a good investment. Excerpts could be used to explain why the NAC chose to do activities in certain ways, and if staff want to learn more, having a KIT for that purpose would be reasonable.

❖ ORGANIZATION AND CONTENT

As indicated in its title, this is Book 1 in the needs assessment KIT. The others are:

Book 2: *Phase I: Getting Started*

Book 3: *Phase II: Collecting Data*

Book 4: *Analysis and Prioritization*

Book 5: *Phase III: Taking Action for Change*

Everything in the KIT is organized around the concept of a three-phase model for needs assessment originated by Witkin (1984), modified by Witkin and Altschuld (1995), Altschuld and Witkin (2000), and now expanded and amended. There are 14 steps in the current version. The first two chapters of this handbook cover an explanation of the concept of need, examples of needs, and the steps in the model. The next four move into a closer look at the phases and how to conduct an assessment study. Chapters 3 through 6 are devoted to the three phases. The last parts of the book contain an outline of a final report, a glossary of terms, and a list of references. In the 2000 book there was an initial glossary that has now grown substantially.

The KIT flows out of this first volume. The second book focuses on getting the effort started via Phase I activities. The third one covers Phase II and is limited to key procedures for collecting assessment data. In Book 4 the content is devoted to analyzing needs data and arriving at needs-based priorities (Phase III). Book 5 deals with translating results into actions for the organization (Phase III) and how it changes as an outgrowth of being involved in the entire process. How has it learned, and how will it continue to learn from this effort as it moves forward? Tied into learning would be the issue of whether this investigation of needs has been evaluated and in what ways subsequent efforts will be conducted, capitalizing upon the strengths and weaknesses of what was just completed.

The KIT is not an encyclopedia of everything about needs assessment. The authors of the books chose useful content and what would generalize to the majority of situations. The specifics of local contexts may require techniques and approaches beyond the coverage provided; in such instances look to the citations throughout the KIT.

❖ SPECIAL FEATURES

The examples in all of the books come from the real world. In this first book, the discussion of several models of assessing needs followed by an expanded examination of the three-phase model is notable since juxtaposition of several models generally is not the case. The glossary of terms as noted is much larger than before.

Additionally, there is a shift in emphasis related to the three-phase model. Originally it was more oriented to a consultant working with an organization to identify and prioritize its needs. Now, the process is seen as externally guided initially, but as it moves into Phase III the work evolves from being externally facilitated and led to being internally directed. The shift is subtle but dramatic. The personnel of organizations, not consultants, implement changes, and hence the shift is necessary to produce staff "buy-in" to needs-based new directions.

Another feature that is emphasized is documenting and evaluating what has been done in every aspect of the process. We have tried to offer simple ways of tracking what has been accomplished. In previous writing these topics were covered superficially. Several novel categories of need are described in the first book. Approximate time parameters are suggested for current and future-oriented needs. Asset (capacity building) assessment is contrasted with traditional needs assessment.

Extensive coverage (Book 2) is given to initiating a study of needs and conducting preassessment activities in order to yield utilitarian and focused results. Without the right start, the process may dissipate and become an exercise in futility. Book 3 helps readers understand how to design and carry out procedures for the assessment phase (Phase II) should it be necessary. A small number of key techniques are explained although there are many that could be used.

In Book 4, the treatment of data and how to derive priorities from multiple sources are described. Book 5 is where the "envelope is pushed." One indicator of a successful assessment is that the organization changes policies or the way it does business. A broader perspective, however, takes into consideration how the organization, through engaging in this work, is becoming a learning environment where growth, development, and exploration are encouraged.

We would be remiss if we did not reflect on a basic premise of needs assessment, which is that there are three levels imbedded in it with Level 1, the recipients of services or products, being foremost. The needs of Level 1 are the *sine qua non* condition for the existence of the organization. They must never be subverted, as they sometimes are, to those of Levels 2 and 3. Moreover, the examination of needs should not be "top-down." When it is, it may only serve to perpetuate the status quo. The formation of an NAC helps alleviate this problem. It should consist of members who have different views and who may come from each of the three levels. The NAC is the guts of all needs assessment activity, and if membership is chosen carefully, it will tend to issues related to not having a Level 1 focus and being "controlled" or manipulated. The importance of the NAC is clear in the KIT.

❖ HOW TO USE THIS BOOK AND THE KIT

Virtually all parties involved with the assessment should read or become familiar with Chapters 1 and 2 of the initial book. They are the storyline of the process, the framework for everyone to see what needs are, what types of needs exist, and what steps are required to probe into their nature. From there, the facilitator should be on a first-name basis with the rest of the chapters—in particular the preassessment phase. It is the launching pad for all subsequent needs-related activity. The members of the NAC should read or skim these chapters as needed. Decision makers and staff should look at ideas as necessary or if they desire to learn more. This pattern would be repeated with regard to the entire KIT with the facilitator being on top of content and ideas. The KIT was designed for flexible use—view it that way.

Acknowledgments

This KIT was a major undertaking and could only result from the work and input of many individuals. Thanks to all the researchers and needs assessors who shared their experiences with us directly or through writing. Many graduate students at The Ohio State University (OSU) have over the years interacted with the first author and influenced his thinking in powerful and seductive ways. They are cited via citations or acknowledgments. Three recent students, Jane Evans, Yi-Fang Lee, and Jeffry White, are additionally thanked for their help.

Our coauthors helped make the dream of a KIT emerge in reality. Gratitude goes to Nick Eastmond of Utah State University, Jean King of the University of Minnesota, Laurel Stevahn of Seattle University, and Jeff White of University of Louisiana at Lafayette for the diligence, perseverance, and talent they devoted to this assignment.

In this same regard, Barbara Heinlein performed alchemy in turning our lead-like rough, word-processed copy into a fine gold lamé. She has done this on two of the first author's books and now on two of our joint ventures. Let us acknowledge Steve Chambers and Keith Wong at OSU for help with literature searches and assistance with computer problems, respectively.

SAGE has always been a supportive publishing house. In particular, we note C. Deborah Laughton, the first managing editor who initially shepherded this venture for the publisher. While she has moved to another venue she was instrumental in the early thinking about this KIT. Then Lisa Cuevas Shaw, Marge Grouppen, and Karen Wong and now Vicki Knight, Sean Connelly, and Lauren Habib followed C. Deborah with the same supportive manner and with the utmost of thought. Their work made the path much smoother. The diligence of Melinda Masson (our copy editor) and Brittany Bauhaus (the production editor) has enhanced this work immensely. To all of you noted above please accept our fondest regards.

Working on a KIT requires a great investment of time and many lonely and long hours. It would not have been possible without the love of our families. For the Altschulds there is Ruth, Steven (Karen, Andrew, and Lindsay), and David (Gina Signoracci). Your love and understanding have been wonderful. On the Kumar side, Satya Oliver and Rachel Jasper made a difference across the seas. Lastly, Belle Ruth Witkin (1918–1998) serves as an inspiration, and her ideas still resonate with us. She was ahead of her time. Belle Ruth, thank you so much!

The authors and SAGE gratefully acknowledge the contributions of the following reviewers:

Jody Bortone, *Sacred Heart University*

Stephanie Brzuzy, *Xavier University*

Ellen Darden, *Concord University*

Laura Nichols, *Santa Clara University*

Diane E. Schmidt, *California State University, Chico*

Wendy L. Wolfersteig, *Arizona State University*

About the Authors

James W. Altschuld, PhD, received his bachelor's and master's degrees in chemistry from Case Western Reserve University and The Ohio State University (OSU), respectively. His doctorate is from the latter institution with an emphasis on educational research and development and sociological methods. He is now professor emeritus in the College of Education and Human Ecology at OSU after 27 years of teaching research techniques and program evaluation. In evaluation, he developed and taught a sequence of courses on theory, needs assessment, and design. He has coauthored three previous books (two on needs assessment and the other on the evaluation of science and technology education), has written many chapters on needs assessment as well as others on evaluation research and issues, and has an extensive list of publications, almost all in the field of evaluation. He has given presentations and done work in five countries outside of the United States. In his career he has been the recipient of local, state, and national honors including the Alva and Gunnar Myrdal Practice Award from the American Evaluation Association for contributions to evaluation.

David Devraj Kumar, EdD, is professor of science education at Florida Atlantic University. He earned his doctorate in science education from Vanderbilt University and a master's in analytical chemistry from the University of Louisville. He has been associate dean of research and graduate studies in education at Florida Atlantic University, a postdoctoral fellow at The Ohio State University, and a guest scholar at The Brookings Institution. His research interests include hypermedia learning environments, science-technology-society studies, evaluation, and policy. His publications include refereed journal articles and books. He has received numerous awards and recognitions for his teaching and research. He is an elected Fellow of the American Association for the Advancement of Science.

1

Beginnings

❖ WHY A KIT?

Much is known about needs assessment with many good sources available, so is this KIT really needed? Yet there is not a single location where a needs assessor can go for the full enterprise with some depth of focus—a place that provides comprehensive guidance and procedures for carrying out a needs assessment. Comprehensive means tables, examples, action steps, and techniques for conducting the assessment from initial conceptualization to identification and prioritization of needs, causal analysis of the problems underlying needs, utilization of results for needs-based action plans in organizations, recycling back to the process as necessary, and lastly evaluation of the endeavor.

Another reason for a KIT is that needs assessments often are not conducted as they should be in that they do not include the two basic conditions of a need (what should be and what is), and beyond that they do not lead to organizational change (actions, ways of thinking), prompting the question as to why they were undertaken in the first place. The process frequently has been treated in a piecemeal and fragmented fashion and to a high degree still is. Training for the conduct of assessments follows this pattern with it usually taught as a small part of an evaluation or planning course. It doesn't receive the attention due to something so important, so potentially troublesome, and as utilitarian as it is. Because assessing needs is associated with evaluation, it is expected that instruction about it would be prominent in evaluation training programs. This is not the case (Engle & Altschuld, 2003/2004; Engle, Altschuld, & Kim, 2006). Surveys of the 29 programs identified in 2006 led to only one full needs assessment course, and it was offered by the first author of this book. In a prior study (Altschuld, Engle, Cullen, Kim, & Macce, 1994) only four relevant courses were found in 49 evaluation programs, and two of them were by the same author. Clearly, a training gap for needs assessment exists.

By extension, a gap in the practice of needs assessment (Figure 1.1) occurs (Altschuld & Witkin, 2000). It generally starts with the best of intentions only to dissipate, especially if it runs long. The effects of an assessment may be muted and below expectations because of inadequate planning, not understanding what is involved, and not integrating it into the deliberation and decision-making processes of the organization.

Figure 1.1   The Gap in Needs Assessment Practice

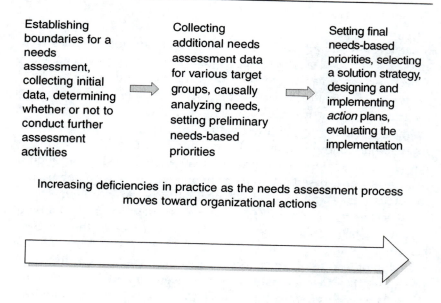

Source: From *From Needs Assessment to Action: Transforming Needs Into Solution Strategies,* by J. W. Altschuld and B. Witkin, 2000, Thousand Oaks, CA: Sage. Used with permission.

With this perspective in mind, this KIT provides an applied understanding of needs assessment and a fairly complete set of procedures and tools for those who conduct the activity. It will be valuable for individuals versed in the topic and equally useful for others who are less familiar with it but who may be assigned to do this type of study in their workplace. The KIT is user friendly with hands-on strategies and examples imbedded in its five books, and at the same time it grounds the reader in the principles of assessing needs.

❖ WHAT IS THE INTENT OF THIS BOOK?

This book contains basic concepts related to needs and needs assessment. It emphasizes a three-phase model for conducting an assessment. A number of methods are given in enough detail to implement them or get a good sense of their main features. The other handbooks contain more of the specifics of methods and processes.

❖ WHAT IS NEED?

Informally, need implies a problem that should be attended to or resolved. Something is missing, wrong, or not working right, and action must be taken to deal with this troubling situation. A discrepancy is perceived—activities are not taking place in the way we think they should. Formally, need is the measurable gap between two conditions—"what is" (the current status or state) and "what should be" (the desired status or state). The two conditions must be measured and the discrepancy between them determined. Not doing so means that we have not directly identified a need. Inherent in needs is the idea that we must go beyond discrepancies to rectify factors causing needs. The simple definition becomes complex when probed.

First, *need* in grammatical usage is a noun, not a verb. If used as a verb, confusion will result. Consider the following:

"Students in the second grade need more time and drill in mathematics to achieve higher scores on their proficiency tests."

This sentence looks like a need but isn't one; it's a solution strategy. It has a sense of a problem or need but not a measured discrepancy. The implied gap is that students are not achieving in math. But the need has not been ascertained by comparing "what should be" and "what is," and data regarding the conditions probably have not been collected.

Also recognize that there could be many solutions—improved teacher training, newer and better mathematics materials to facilitate student work, altered instructional approaches, and different content and curricula. Time and drill are one solution to a problem that has not been elucidated and examined in depth. We could implement any of the solutions, but the problem could relate to a different aspect of mathematics achievement, thus wasting valuable resources. The need and its cause(s) have not been fully clarified.

The distinction between solution and need is important, and it affects the needs assessment process. Groups tend to jump prematurely to solutions before identifying and prioritizing needs or delving into what underlies them. It is part of us as doers. We don't want to be slowed down; rather we want to focus on solutions. Needs, not solutions, have to be the concern, and groups must be kept on target, thinking first about needs; otherwise poor or unfitting solutions could be implemented at considerable cost in time, energy, and fiscal resources. A task for the facilitator of a needs assessment is to keep a group focused as it gets started. (More about this is provided in Book 2 of the KIT and Chapter 3 of this one.)

A second concern about the definition is that often studies are mislabeled as needs assessments. In work done by Witkin (personal communication, 1994) and students in our classes, many such so-called investigations only deal with one of the two essential conditions. Perhaps 60%–70% of all articles are of this nature. They are ways for sensing problems or getting an idea of a direction for a program or project, but they are not needs assessments. Discrepancies have not been determined. (Despite this we strongly endorse the use of the literature for methods and examples of instruments.)

In some instances, need is inferred or sensed—"Tell us what you think is needed" (a solution approach)—instead of "Help us to delineate discrepancies targeted for action." Needs sensing (Lewis, 2006) is cheaper, quicker, and easier to conduct, but at best it is only about implied gaps. While of value, it falls short of what we see as a needs assessment.

Third, in some situations the "what should be" condition is easy to state, and for others it is quite variable. Body temperature presents no particular difficulty for a "what should be" state—98.6 degrees Fahrenheit or thereabouts is an appropriate standard. For cholesterol, the "what should be" is below 200 for total cholesterol, and the ratio of total to high-density lipids should be less than 4.5. As cholesterol rises above 200 and the ratio exceeds 4.5, the risk of heart problems increases. Research has established the "what should be." Continuing in health, "Healthy People 2010" has specified evidence-based program outcomes for the United States such as increasing life expectancy and reducing the number of new cancer cases (U.S. Department of Health and Human Services, 2005).

Other areas are not like this, with the "what should be" value-driven. What should be the outcomes of a high school education? Should graduates be familiar with a second language and have a certain level of proficiency in it as is desirable in Portugal, Belgium, and other countries? What should a high school student understand about science by the 12th grade? Even in health, what does it mean to be well, and what are expectations for wellness (physical conditioning, diet, mental health, upper body strength) for Americans (by age, gender, and ethnic group) or for another country (and strata within it)?

Going further, the "what should be" may be vague and lacking in clarity. Consider the social studies books used in many American schools. Some educators see them as watered down in content and language and mired in political correctness (Archibald, 2004). If this is accurate, what should the content be, how should it be chosen, who should have approval, how should sensitive historical events (slavery, the war in Vietnam, the Holocaust, My Lai, the sadness of Nanking) be portrayed, and at what level of difficulty should the books be written? Arriving at standards for language and the subtle dimensions of textbooks is tenuous given that many voices shape the debate and decisions regarding development and selection. Agreeing on "what should be" is more difficult than specifying a desirable level of cholesterol.

Another factor affecting the "what should be" condition is the wording of questions on needs assessment surveys. Is it "what ought to be," "what ideally should be," "what is likely to be," "what is expected to be," "what is feasible," "what is minimally acceptable," or "what might be the normative expectation"? These are scales from actual surveys and may not lead to the same results. Limited research has been done about which type works best with different groups and whether variations affect the outcomes of assessment studies.

Adding to the issue, is it appropriate to stress the "ideal" frame in questions? The argument is that we should strive for the ideal rather than for lesser outcomes. Would we have gone to the moon if we had aimed for figuratively lower objectives? Does it make sense to emphasize minimal competency for educational systems? If so, is that all we would attain and nothing more? Should that be the goal for educational and social programs? On the other hand, it may be better to not raise hopes and instead focus on what is achievable or likely or to use several levels of the "what should be" on surveys to encourage respondents to think about multiple possibilities. How then should we structure items on needs assessment surveys? This is a perplexing conceptual and practical concern. The wording that we use on surveys reflects our values.

Choices have to be made, and different wordings probably lead to varied perceptions of need. We could wind up dealing not with true needs ("true" is an elusive idea) but with something referred to as wants or wishes. Needs assessors should be sensitive to how instrumentation impacts the process and interpretations of needs data. Unfortunately, there are few investigations about the design of surveys, how to frame items, and the length of time that survey results about needs remain viable (Hamann, 1997; Lee, 2005; Lee, Altschuld, & White, 2007b; Malmsheimer & Germain, 2002).

❖ EXAMPLES OF NEEDS

In Table 1.1, examples of needs (with one want) are provided. Two "what should be" states are shown, illustrating some of the considerations woven into needs assessment. Most of the entries relate to organizations that deliver services and products to individuals and groups.

Needs assessments are undertaken by organizations, hopefully with a focus on the needs of those they serve in order to improve services and products for their clientele. Needs here are collective, not those of individuals (Maslow, 1970). Because organizations carry out the process, don't assume that a top-down approach is being advocated or that groups and individuals are seen as targets. The needs of the organization must pertain to those who receive its services or products. The needs of students, the unemployed, patients, and clients (Level 1 needs) should always govern organizational actions.

Needs assessments are done by schools; health agencies; the extension service; libraries; local, state, and federal agencies; municipal service providers; charities; and businesses. Mostly, organizations have the resources required—human, fiscal, administrative, and other support. (Because of this, sometimes assessments purportedly done for Level 1 are in reality those of Level 2, service providers.)

This means that the facilitator(s) of the process must intimately know the organization for which the assessment is being conducted. They must be familiar with its characteristics and how it goes about accomplishing day-to-day activities. They should get a feel for the under-the-surface and hidden nuances of procedures and policies. They should learn about how decisions are made, formal and informal

Table 1.1 Examples of the "What Is," "What Ideally Should Be," and "What Is Likely" States

Area	What Is	What Ideally Should Be	What Is Likely
Health	30% of U.S. population is overweight	100% at or near a reasonable weight for age, height, gender, and body build	75% will reach the standard within a 5-year period
Mathematics	62.8% of district students achieve the state standard for the fourth-grade mathematics test	100% reach the standard or 75% reach the standard to remove the district from possible state sanctions	65% or more achieve the standard by this time next year
Reading	75% of eighth-grade students understand the instructions on an aspirin bottle or a package of patent medicine	100% should be able to do the task	85% are able to do the task 2 years from now after exposure to improved reading instruction
Youth Recreation	A community does not have a recreation center and adequate recreation activities for youth	A recreation center will be built and open 5 years from now Within 1 year a recreation program will be started in the community	The recreation center will be a reality 10 years from now A small recreation program will start in 2 years and slowly expand
Immunization	The inoculation rate for preschool children in a particular state is currently at 70%–75%	A rate of 90%–95% will be achieved, thus reducing the likelihood of the incidence (spread) of certain diseases	Rate of inoculation will slowly increase to 80% over a 5-year period Rate will remain the same without the causes of the problem being understood

(Continued)

Table 1.1 (Continued)

Area	What Is	What Ideally Should Be	What Is Likely
Wealth	An individual is currently worth $1,000,000	With inflation and worries about job stability the individual would prefer to be at $2,000,000 to feel more secure	$1,500,000 would be likely in light of the general growth of investments within a 10-year period
Driving While Under the Influence	9% of all drivers during the period from 1 a.m. to 4 a.m. on weekend nights are above the legal limit for intoxication	Nearly 0% with rigorous law enforcement procedures, more sobriety checkpoints, and stiffer penalties	3%–4% even with the procedures specified in the previous column
Educational System	Current state standards for courses and areas required for a high school degree	Given changes in knowledge and the world of work, what standards should we develop for children now entering the educational system and who graduate in 13 years?	What are reasonable expectations for change in complex multidimensional systems like education?

influences, empowerment and support of staff, and what the overall demeanor feels like. To help the facilitator(s) in this overall task, the text periodically contains lists of questions for guiding the assessment.

Needs assessments have an impact on what organizations do and how they change. They may affect (possibly upset) power structures and the delicate balance that is critical for effectiveness. Needs assessors must go beyond the technical aspects of procedures, which, although important, are far from enough. A technically successful study of needs could be a failure if it does not become a part of the organizational mindset and lead to improvement and action. (See Altschuld, 2004, for a more in-depth discussion of this point.) This is brought out in the situation described below (see Example 1.1).

Example 1.1

Failure to Assess the Organizational Climate for Needs Assessment

An external team conducted a needs assessment for a nationwide consortium of businesses and an engineering department in a major university. It was partly supported by the state in which the university was located. The goal was to identify training needs and to recommend educational initiatives for the engineering field. The consortium was guided by an advisory council made up of member businesses.

A nationwide Delphi study (iterative surveys) was implemented with the involvement of engineers who initially were skeptical of this social science effort but in time became major and enthusiastic supporters of it. Toward the end of the project, the administration of the consortium changed with a dramatic and noticeable shift in direction, relegating the project to the back burner.

While the study produced excellent and meaningful results, the new administrators were polite but less than avid about following up on them. They conveyed their feelings to the advisory council, and things went nowhere. About 2 years later, the needs assessors learned that the consortium recognized that an opportunity to earn millions of dollars had been missed due to not heeding the results.

The assessment was a technical success but a real-world failure. What is the lesson to be learned from this experience? It is to be vigilant to the changing dimensions and tone in the consortium and to establish and maintain channels of communication. They are not automatically there, and it was incumbent on the needs assessors in this instance to re-create them. This action may not have saved the needs assessment, but this example demonstrates the importance of communication.

Returning to Table 1.1, "what ideally should be" and "what is likely" are depicted (but other possibilities for wording could be used). The needs assessor(s) and those involved in the process must be clear about this condition and what they are after when assessing needs.

There is variation in how expectations can be stated as in the last two columns for the Mathematics, Youth Recreation, and Immunization rows. There are different, value-laden "what should be" statements in the cells. Thinking about this, responses to scaled survey questions could be quite disparate for constituent groups who come from unique perspectives and who could, in extreme cases, be diametrically opposed. Results depend on the subtlety of wording and interpretation by responding groups.

Other aspects of needs are included in the table. The Wealth entry satisfies the definition of need but is a want, not a need. Noting this distinction, Scriven and Roth (1978, 1990) modified the definition of need to help in separating the two. In their view, a rule to follow is a "reasonable person" stance for deciding whether a need does or does not exist. The reasonable person would say that while the discrepancy from $1,000,000 to $2,000,000 fits the definition of need, it is not one. It goes beyond a satisfactory state of financial security and is a want. Conversely, wealthy people could see it as a need from their vantage point. The relative nature of needs is obvious. Values are in play and have an impact on the majority of needs assessments and on the final selection and prioritization of needs.

❖ TIME DIMENSIONS FOR NEEDS

The last row in the table is a long-term or future-oriented type of need. All needs are future oriented, but some are of a more short-term duration and others of a much longer term. There are no prescriptions that govern what is short- and long-term. Arbitrarily, "short-term" denotes a period of 3 years or less (emphasis on less) into the future with the implication that the needs could be resolved in that time frame. More than 3 years would be the longer term.

The time is noteworthy especially in education. School leaders (high-level administrators) in big-city school systems tend to have a limited tenure, perhaps 3–4 years, and may not be in the school district after that period. There is turnover of other staff during the same time span, and the membership of committees that look at needs and guide the assessment changes with a loss of institutional and committee history. Due to this, leaders and others may be reluctant or unwilling to attend to or deal with long-term needs. Why stake reputations on the long term when they might not be there to receive credit for problem resolution? It is difficult to make a commitment to the long term, putting one's energy and spirit into it. Business may be like education with leaders feeling short-term pressure about the bottom line at the expense of the longer term, keeping in mind that the latter entails a lot of uncertainty, especially as we project into the future. The nearer-term mentality is prevalent despite the fact that some problems are complicated and seemingly intractable. Think of drug addiction, poverty, road and infrastructure development, transportation concerns, alcoholism, smoking and its effects on health, maintenance and upgrading of electrical power systems, and our reliance on fossil fuels and foreign sources of them. In such instances the short-term fixes and term mentality are not appropriate.

Furthermore, it is difficult to maintain organizational memory in needs assessment studies, especially for long-term needs. It is for this reason that minutes of meetings, forms and data collection instruments, reports, recommendations for action and actions taken, and so on be saved for evaluation purposes and input into subsequent investigations of needs (see Example 1.2).

Example 1.2

The Perils of Long-Term Needs

In an interesting article titled "The Future of Jobs: New Ones Arise, Wage Gap Widens," Wessel (2004) examined projections in areas expected to lose the most jobs between 1998 and 2000 made by the Bureau of Labor Statistics. When compared to the actual numbers lost, the projections had startling variability. In some cases the estimates were fairly accurate, whereas in others expected losses did not approach the magnitude of the actual ones (61,000 losses anticipated in word processors and typists vs. 503,000 jobs that disappeared; 89,000 losses anticipated in garment and sewing machine operators vs. 324,000 jobs that disappeared). At the same time 384,000 jobs were created for hand packers and packagers when it was anticipated 75,000 jobs would be gone.

Wessel (2004) pointed out the complexity and hazard of long-term projections in jobs and employment. Projective techniques are fraught with assumptions and prone to error. In terms of jobs they are subject to a rapidly changing workplace and economic conditions not only in the United States but throughout the world.

❖ TOO MANY ISSUES

Too many issues have been raised, there's too much to deal with, and needs assessment seems to be a morass of values and issues. But understanding what may be involved helps in doing a better job of assessing needs. The issues point toward the careful consideration, purposeful decision making, and planning that must occur in assessment to make for outcomes of merit and worth to an organization. They alert you to what might or could occur.

Even small endeavors and certainly large ones necessitate pre-assessment activity before being started. Needs assessments can (but do not always) consume much time, money, and human investment. If not handled well, they can lead to acrimony over perspectives that at worst are on opposite ends of the spectrum within and across groups. They can exacerbate and accentuate differences instead of building on strengths and commonalities. They may be confrontational if not handled with a nurturing attitude. (Questions imbedded in many procedures will be helpful in uncovering conflicts and working with a needs assessment committee to resolve them.)

Assessments can drag on interminably. They can drain a creative group of its interest, willingness, *joie de vivre* (*esprit de corps*), and commitment. Fervor for change and improvement at the beginning can rapidly disappear. People, even those who are into the process, may get bored (the maturation source of invalidity from Campbell & Stanley, 1963) with the whole thing and "turn off," leaving the endeavor to die slowly on the vine.

All of these things do happen. The needs assessor should be aware of what might go wrong and, by taking such into account, design and implement a better process, one more likely to lead to change. Snags can be avoided or reduced. A good assessment plan eases the path to quality results that will be utilized and appreciated by the organization.

❖ WHY ARE NEEDS IMPORTANT?

Why should we care about this idea of need? To begin, Hansen (1991) found that assessing needs is a universal activity across health, engineering, education, and other fields. Sometimes the word *need* (with substitutes such as *problem, gap, deficiency, discrepancy, issue,* or *concern*) is not used, but procedures in diverse disciplines are, predicated on the discrepancy between "what is" and "what should be." Needs are important because they make us consider risk factors in regard to them.

Needs are problems confronting organizations, groups, and societies (e.g., terrorism, economic competition via outsourcing, challenges to ways of life). In them are elements of risk, and once a need is identified it will be useful to analyze risks (negative consequences) that might be incurred by not attending or attending to it. Can they be tolerated? Needs assessment and risk assessment are highly interwoven, and ideally both should be assessed.

In epidemiology, risks are estimated and factored into decisions for prevention programs. Epidemiologists refer to prevalence—the current number of individuals and/or animals having a disease (such as AIDS, influenza, the two forms of diabetes, SARS, chronic wasting disease in wild herds, or avian flu)—and the incidence—the number of individuals who will get the disease in the future. Prevalence and incidence are indicators of risk with the latter pointing to whether or not we are facing an epidemic. Prevalence and incidence are critical to deciding what should be done to keep populations healthy by lowering or stopping the rate of spread of diseases.

Reduction of risk is essential for the maintenance of health. Risk is used by insurance companies and government agencies. It is input for policies regarding the health of aging populations, the consumption of natural resources, and so forth. In these fields, it may be easier to estimate risk than in education, social programming, community infrastructure, criminology, and recreation. In recreation it is hard to portray what might be associated with decisions to add or not add recreational facilities and gyms in cities and neighborhoods. Would the crime rate decrease with more of these, or might it increase by providing a convenient location for some groups to meet? If facilities were not under consideration, how could the risks associated with not attending to the morale and psychological needs of citizens be determined?

What are the consequences of not all students achieving grade level in reading (or mathematics) when probably the majority of them will productively work and contribute to the economic well-being of a country or region? (So they don't do well on higher-level math concepts—does that materially affect the majority of jobs and work situations?) What is the risk of recidivism when convicted felons are paroled? To what degree will sex offenders and pedophiles revert to past behavior, and what kinds of follow-up services would be necessary to prevent this? Risks should be part of the criteria used when rating options for programmatic decisions when going from the assessment of need to actions for organizations. Along these lines, Altschuld and Witkin (2000) posited 10 types of risk in needs assessment divided into two categories (internal and external to the organization).

Let us return to the main question, "Is need important?" Given that there is risk in not meeting a need, it is—especially since needs guide so many of our collective activities.

❖ WAYS TO CLASSIFY NEEDS

In Table 1.2, classes are given. (Other classifications are possible. As one illustration, Bradshaw, in 1972, posited categories such as normative

Table 1.2 Types of Needs

Type	Characteristics	Comments
Present (Short-Term) Versus Future (Long-Term)	Some needs are short-term in nature (3 years or less with emphasis on less) Long-term needs will generally be over 3 years or more into the future	Groups will focus more easily on short-term needs (i.e., ones that they can see being resolved in lesser periods of time) Longer-term needs will be difficult to mobilize support for and to develop commitment of groups to their resolution
Severe Versus Slight	Some needs will be considered to be severe (larger in scope or of more consequence) Others will be of not so great scope and not represent as great an underlying problem	Severe or major problems will be more complex, will be harder to deal with and resolve, will take more time and resources for resolution, etc. As in the prior row, it will be easier to develop enthusiasm for solving slight needs
Maintenance/Upgrade	Does not indicate a direct discrepancy at the current time but will become a need if a service, level of skill, etc., is not maintained or upgraded	All systems and skills need maintenance, which if neglected will lead to problems (discrepancies)
Collaborative	Needs assessments carried out by collaboration between two (bilateral) or more (multilateral) cooperating institutions or agencies	Organizations sense or feel that collaboratively (mutually) assessing needs and solving them have advantages for each involved agency and institution
Levels 1 (Recipients of Services), 2 (Deliverers of Services), and 3 (System Supporting Levels 1 and 2)	Level 1 deals with needs of those who receive services, Level 2 focuses on those who deliver services and what they require to do so, and Level 3 relates to overall needs (funds, facilities, etc.) of the system to support Level 2 and, in turn, Level 1	Many times are carried out at the second or third levels rather than at the first one Level 1 is to be stressed since it is the reason for the existence of Levels 2 and 3

(Continued)

Table 1.2 (Continued)

Type	Characteristics	Comments
Asset or Capacity Building	Approaching the issue not from a discrepancy point of view but from that of building and capitalizing upon assets and strengths rather than deficits or needs	Needs assessment always starts with needs or problems instead of strengths It is more positive to think about the strengths of the community and how to use them than to focus on needs (negatives)
Retrospective	Retrospective needs are assessed generally after a project or a program is underway and is at the point of undergoing a summative evaluation. If there has not been a prior needs assessment or if questions arise as to what or whose needs are being served, then the situation might call for a retrospective assessment of needs	In general, retrospective assessments of need are not often seen in the literature. An early citation is in the Program Evaluation Kit (1978) as suggested by Herman, Morris, and Fitz-Gibbon used in conjunction with the evaluation of a program This may be a catch-up mechanism when the need for a project was not established previously or an unanticipated or different Level 1 group than intended is utilizing project resources

needs, those where the "what should be" comes from research as in some facets of health care; felt needs, those that members of a group express they have; and others.)

When starting to work with an advisory group guiding the assessment, clarity as to type of need is helpful in establishing a common framework. Groups and individuals ascribe different meanings to the word, and time can be lost in handling disagreements. Being clear at the start makes the needs assessment flow smoothly and creates a more task-oriented environment. Therefore, it is recommended that the facilitator(s) explain critical terms and ideas.

The time frame for a need is important as is whether it is severe or slight. Attention and commitment to short-term, slight needs will usually be more obtainable than to long-term, severe ones, which take more resources and effort to resolve with potential loss of interest over time. Contrast the need to upgrade basic skills in the use of spreadsheets to the training required to manipulate complex relational databases. The former is easier and less costly. The concern with long- versus short-term and severe versus slight needs was stressed by Witkin in 1984. She described a collaborative needs assessment, a table entry, conducted by four agencies (county government, local and county school systems, and a local municipality) for youth in an area. It was conducted by a committee of representatives from the four agencies with procedures tailored to fit various stakeholder groups. The representatives were the needs assessment committee (NAC)—a policy-making board for the assessment and a working one that may collect some of the data. The assessment was a classic with the use of multiple methods as advocated by many authors.

The needs assessment, although a methodological success, was nevertheless unsuccessful. Murphy's law took hold, and what could go wrong did, with the normal problems being multiplied by four. Learning, wisdom, and guidance come from failures. In Witkin's (1984) analysis of why things went wrong and what should be done in future assessments, she postulated a set of ideas pertinent to several rows in the table:

- Focus on short-term needs initially; otherwise long-term ones will reduce the commitment of NAC members and their organizations.

- Identify needs of high priority to all involved organizations (but not necessarily the top one for a single organization) that hopefully they can agree to.

- Focus on needs that can be quickly resolved (a partial outgrowth of the first idea).

- Make sure that there are ties to the informal and formal decision-making structures of the organizations.

She encouraged us to think about the distinctions between short- and long-term needs and severe and slight needs. In collaborative endeavors these contrasts are magnified in importance and will be critical for a positive outcome. The idea is that success breeds success and creates the foundation for further work in mutually resolving problems. By dealing with short-term problems, the good the collaborative can accomplish becomes evident, and the value in joining forces and the empowerment to deal with more severe, long-term needs grow. Once short-term results are in hand, redirect attention to the longer-term, more severe needs. At any rate, it is wise to heed Witkin's (1984) observations arising from the crucible of experience.

Returning to the table, maintenance needs of mechanical systems, the human body and health, societal infrastructure, and educational systems are sometimes lost in the "needs assessment shuffle" but should not be. If not maintained, automobiles, airplanes, and computer and mechanical systems decay and eventually fail. Suppose computers or the Internet were to break down, be hacked into, or be attacked by a pernicious virus. What would happen to our daily lives if the systems were not maintained? How much of existence is controlled by or dependent on these means—would we be able to pay bills, invest, take a plane to see relatives (we probably would not even get off the ground), make a reservation, and so on? The situation would be intolerable.

Maintenance needs sometimes appear when a service is altered or changed such as when people retire and find that they no longer have certain aspects of previous medical coverage. In this situation the resources for coverage have to be reallocated from one's pocket whereas before they were from medical plans.

Associated with maintenance needs are upgrades of systems. Look at the blackout of 2003, which went from the eastern United States and Canada all the way into Ohio and left as many as 50,000,000 people without electric power, or Hurricane Ike in 2008. Was the equipment maintained and up-to-date? (One of the authors lives in an area with several major outages a year, probably due to an inadequate and outdated system despite protestations to the contrary by the electric company.)

The same rationale applies to the human body and health. We need to exercise although no immediate need may be apparent. The subtle effects of obesity, diet, and lack of exercise accumulate over time. When we stay in shape, better health is ensured as is fuller recovery from health problems that occur with the normal process of aging. Analogously, adherence to pharmaceutical regimens is also crucial. Further, consider the current and alarming rise in type 1 (childhood onset) and type II (adult onset) diabetes, and the need for health maintenance becomes prominent. The impact on the health care costs of not attending to maintenance needs for this single disease over 10 or 15 years will be extremely high. It will affect the health care costs of all of us (Chiasera, 2005), whether we are afflicted with it or not.

Maintenance needs may not be very appealing to deal with, put emphasis on, or make one's mark within an institution. We may not want to think about using limited resources for maintenance concerns; they seem mundane and elicit limited excitement and fervor, but neglecting them, especially over the long haul, can be perilous. The facilitator of the needs assessment must be attuned to the subtlety of such needs and if appropriate alert the NAC to what might happen if they are not given full attention.

The sixth row in Table 1.2 is a counterpoint to much of the previous discussion. Some perceive that in needs there is a sense of the negative, that the focus is on problems and what's wrong. In working with community needs that sense can be discouraging; it may sour things and not motivate individuals to action. Wouldn't it be more sensible to look at strengths and resources and how they can be expanded upon and mobilized? Community strengths reside in cultural, ecological, social, economic, and spiritual resources.

In assessments of the asset base, members of a community may be active in conceptualizing what is done and intimately involved in the data collection process. They may participate in decisions about what information is necessary based upon their knowledge of the environment. They would help in compiling lists of community assets, which are the linchpin for planning and activity. Even though decisions still have to be made about how to effectively deploy community resources, the starting point is radically different than it is in traditional needs assessment. Asset or capacity building is a legitimate concern. An assessment may be implemented so that it doesn't dwell on negatives and, if done in combination with a capacity stance, could be an excellent strategy for improvement. The idea of leveraging what is there could be easily incorporated into the overall process.

The last row in the table deals with a seeming self-contradiction—retrospective needs. If needs assessment occur at the start of an endeavor, why should there be a retrospective form of the endeavor? A retrospective one is different from periodically revisiting or reexamining needs. It is wise for organizations to routinely reconsider what they have done before and the needs they have previously uncovered. A retrospective needs assessment is a bit different. Suppose that in evaluating a project, a sense emerged that the original study had missed the mark or that groups targeted for services were not those who really benefited. This is exactly the case as described below (see Example 1.3).

Example 1.3

Retrospective Needs Assessment

A large suburban school district was worried about students who fall between the cracks, not achieving and fitting in with the majority of college-bound students in the district. Basing their decision upon perceptions of need without having fully investigated the problem, administrators convinced the school board to allocate district funds for after-school academic assistance for middle and high school students. Qualified substitute teachers were hired to staff the program, and it was advertised to teachers, students, and guidance counselors. Student usage numbers were substantial, but something was amiss.

When attendance was assessed from the program database, it was noted that lesser numbers of low-performing students were participating and much greater numbers of the B−, B, and B+ students were involved. A mini retrospective and informal needs assessment was conducted with the result being that the B type of students saw the program as a way to improve their qualifications whereas other students had given up, saw no way to really improve, or just had a relatively poor self-image (i.e., the program helped those for whom it was not intended).

Retrospective assessments are not often seen in the literature and usually are linked to outcome evaluations. They serve as a check on the nature of the need upon which an effort was based and whether the target population was the actual recipient of services.

Finally for Table 1.2, one other possible entry relates to technology and how rapidly technological change can create needs. The Sony Walkman is an exemplar. It was a clever invention with no apparent need or rationale behind it. It seemed like a fun thing to do (not that fun isn't purposeful), but what was it supposed to accomplish? Who would use it, and why would they do so? Now, the Walkman is ubiquitous (as are newer incarnations such as iPods). We see joggers and people who are exercising use it to listen to music, the news, and so forth. Painters and secretaries use it to alleviate the boredom and tedium of their job. Most of these individuals would probably indicate that it is a necessity. This demonstrates what might be called technology pull—the technology was produced and subsequent needs, which we did not know of or could not have ever imagined, appeared. The new technology created the need.

We could also envision a technological innovation pushing needs further than we had thought or understood at its inception. Word processing is a good case of this. Word processing software was developed to improve how manuscripts are generated. It forced one of us, a two-finger typist, to completely change his approach to writing. In other words, technology exposed needs that were only comprehended at a surface level and whose implications were partially sensed or understood. As we became more familiar with the technology, only then did it propel major change.

❖ NEEDS ASSESSMENT: WHAT IS IT?

Needs assessment is the process of identifying needs, prioritizing them, making needs-based decisions, allocating resources, and implementing actions in organizations to resolve problems underlying important needs. When we identify and work on needs, decisions about how resources are allocated have to be made. Unless new resources can be located, ones already there (human, fiscal, material) will be reallocated from one part of the workplace to another. Biblically, somebody's ox will be gored if he or she cannot or will not shift his or her thinking to new, needs-based priorities. There may be losers and winners once the assessment is completed and action plans are implemented. Feathers may be ruffled, and rancor can result. Needs assessment is political, and by attending to politics throughout the process, the likelihood of success will increase. Communication and involvement within the organization have to be structured into the process of assessment. Everyone should be in the loop to ensure greater attention to the process and results.

Needs assessments may be conducted informally by small groups of people, but mostly they are organizational (businesses, community agencies, government institutions) endeavors. There are numerous models or approaches for assessing needs. The Organizational Elements Model (OEM) of Kaufman (1987) focuses on three basic levels of needs or discrepancies as shown in Figure 1.2. The model and elements within it are prominent in human performance technology, and the reader is directed to Altschuld and Lepicki (2009a, 2009b, in press); Clark (2005); McGriff (2003); Watkins and Wedman (2003); Wedman (2007); and the World Bank Institute (2007) Web site with which Watkins has been involved, which has an overview of models.

The external or Mega level represents the needs of society in terms of human development (psychological, economic, physical well-being, etc.). They must be assessed first, followed by the Macro level, which

Figure 1.2   Organizational Element Model

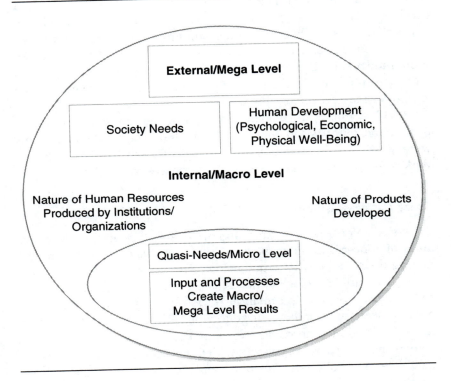

deals with the human resources produced or products generated by institutions and organizations as they relate to attaining Mega level results. For example, the Macro level focuses on how well individuals are being prepared to be productive contributors to society. Such considerations are critical for a country to survive and prosper in an ever-changing world. The Micro level looks at inputs and resources and the processes through which organizations produce Macro and, in turn, Mega level results. Earlier, Kaufman (1987) referred to these levels with the terms *external* (Mega), *internal* (Macro), and *quasi-needs* (Micro).

OEM is an action-based approach to dealing with needs. Along the Mega, Macro, and Micro continuum, discrepancies between "what should be" and "what is" statuses are determined. Besides the needs or gaps at each point, we should examine what is done right and, hence, what should not be changed. Strengths of the OEM lie in its systems orientation, its clarity in focusing the needs assessment process, and the substantive thinking underlying the three levels.

Another way of characterizing the assessment of needs was proposed by Cohen (1981). From the perspective of social agencies and services, it is divided into two categories, procedures for mobilizing support across stake-holding groups and procedures for resource allocation. For the first category, methods involving the participation of groups are required, and for the second, number-driven, statistical data and analysis of records and archived materials come into play. The two categories may also be used in tandem.

In 1984, Witkin developed a process model that contained three phases and emphasized three levels of need. The model and levels were revisited by Witkin and Altschuld (1995) and by Altschuld and Witkin (2000). Our revised version of the phases is as follows.

Phase I: Preassessment

Phase I consists of getting organized and focusing on potential areas of concern, finding out what is *already known or available*, and making decisions on what is understood with respect to the foci. Phase I is a critical building block of needs assessment. Decisions could be to collect more in-depth information (Phase II), stop any further work because needs are not there, or go to Phase III—planning of strategies to resolve identified needs. Phase I activities lead to a wealth of information about the areas of concern with the possibility that nothing else will have to be collected. This phase mainly takes advantage of existing data.

Phase III: Assessment

Phase II deals with collecting new information based on what hasn't been learned in Phase I. Activities also include determining initial priorities of needs and causally analyzing them as relevant to possible solution strategies. Phase II may require an extensive investment of time, personnel, and resources for the collection of new data.

Phase III: Postassessment

Designing and implementing solutions for high-priority needs and evaluating the results of the solution(s) and the needs assessment process constitute Phase III. Evaluation of the process generally is not done but should be as part of organizational development and change.

Intertwined throughout the phases are three levels of need. Level 1 is the direct recipients of services, Level 2 represents the needs of service providers, and Level 3 is of the system that supports service providers and service recipients. The needs of Level 1 should always be prime in the needs assessment process. Levels 2 and 3 are there to serve Level 1, the individuals who benefit from services, programs, and/or products. The needs associated with Levels 2 and 3 should rarely be placed ahead of those of Level 1. A closer look at the three levels follows:

Level 1 (*the primary level*) consists of students, clients, patients, customers, and so on who receive services or products to resolve their needs.

Level 2 (*the secondary level*) is the individuals or groups who deliver services and products to Level 1 (sometimes Level 2 denotes a treatment provided to a Level 1 group). Teachers, social workers, counselors, health care personnel, librarians, sales personnel, trainers, and others make up this level.

Level 3 (*the tertiary level*) is different from Levels 1 and 2 with a focus on resources and the supportive structure that enable Level 2 to provide services. It includes buildings, facilities, classrooms, transportation systems, salaries and benefits, and the like.

Many times information about all levels is available and accessible from organizational sources (databases, files) waiting to be harvested. Much information about Level 1, service recipients, may be within the system as for students in public schools, patients in hospitals, and inmates. In some cases, members of Level 1 are not within system boundaries (e.g., in mental health where many of those in need of counseling are not receiving assistance, may not be aware of or understand that they have needs, or may not want/value help).

Since needs assessments are often conducted by Level 2 personnel, it is no great surprise that many stress, overtly or implicitly, the concerns of Levels 2 and 3 over those of Level 1, with lip service given to the latter. But remember that organizations, agencies, and businesses are there to resolve the needs of Level 1. This rationale for organizational existence may be obscured by our Level 2 and 3 foci, the press of day-to-day work, and the problems confronting us. We lose sight of this goal sometimes because certain types of data are available (and cheaper) and thus Level 1 needs aren't assessed. They may require more effort, patience, energy, and dollars. The emphasis almost imperceptibly shifts to the needs of Level 2 or Level 3 rather than Level 1. It's easy for this to happen. Consider Example 1.4.

Example 1.4

Level 2 Before Level 1!

A mental health agency in a large city decided to collect data about the mental health problems of people living in the community it served. Survey results obtained and prioritized indicated numerous concerns that would be amenable to family counseling (marital issues, child/parent conflicts, employment concerns and job anxieties since unemployment was growing in the area). These were identified as important, priority needs by the agency counseling staff. The counselors who had been involved in the needs assessment were basically family oriented with their training and experience in that area.

What they missed was that the population in their jurisdiction was rapidly aging, and there were many hidden issues (alcoholism, loneliness, inability to attend to daily concerns, misuse of drugs, substance abuse, fear of aging, economic distress based on fixed incomes, boredom, loss of independence) related to age. Would these problems have been perceived differently if the counselors had greater exposure to and interest in issues associated with aging? Would and should different priorities have been stressed? Had Level 2 needs and what Level 2 personnel could deliver ruled out a different interpretation of results?

As another illustration of misdirection of a need, examine Example 1.5. It shows how we should scrutinize results and ask how they fit with the organization providing service. Needs assessments are conducted by institutions, agencies, and businesses that have their own Level 1 groups; they must focus on them, not other ones. This point may be missed when resources to resolve needs are expended.

Example 1.5

What Group Is Level 1?

A not-for-profit organization devoted to the concerns of senior citizens observed that nationwide too few senior women were regularly receiving mammograms. The organization (which is partially funded by member dues) decided to support a countrywide campaign to increase the rate of screenings by providing resources for the endeavor.

While the national need was there, a question arose as to whether or not it was the need of the Level 1 women who belonged to the organization.

The goal was noble, so why should there be any concern? But the purpose of the organization was to serve its dues-paying members. When this issue was explored (a kind of retrospective needs assessment), it was noted that the women in the organization were more affluent than the overall population and were regularly having mammograms. Obviously, the organization supported a program for a different Level 1 group from its members.

It is possible, when a great deal is understood about Level 1, to treat Level 2 as a pseudo Level 1 group. If a lot is known about instructional strategies for improving reading achievement, Level 2 (the teachers) could be the Level 1 target group. The NAC should be specific as to whose needs are of concern and its choice of a particular level for the assessment.

Although terms differ in the three approaches to needs assessment described above, there is similarity across them, particularly the Kaufman (1987, 1992) and Witkin and Altschuld (1995; Altschuld & Witkin, 2000) models. The concept of discrepancy is paramount, the idea of having a clear focus for the process is apparent, and Level 1 needs are inherent in the Mega needs of Kaufman. Beyond that, numerous techniques for conducting assessments are imbedded in the writings of these authors. So the landscape is well established and accessible, but details about step-by-step procedures are less so.

The three-phase process of Witkin and Altschuld (1995) will be the structure underlying this KIT. In Chapter 2, it is expanded with activities per phase and then followed by chapters that look at each phase specifically. An updated glossary of needs assessment terms, a format for reporting results, and an expanded list of references are included in this book.

❖ CAVEATS

There are things that this KIT will not do. First, not all needs assessment methods will be explained. Witkin and Altschuld (1995) sorted more than 20 methods into three main categories—archived (records, logs, social indicators, and other sources of data), communicative (interactive entities such as small- and large-group meetings and noninteractive ones like surveys and the mailed Delphi technique), and analytical (causal analysis, the determination of risks). Many of these are the subject of books, and information about others may be found through Web or quick literature searches. Given this, what we do is describe the main methods in sufficient depth for use and application. We tie them into the needs assessment context and show how they have been adopted and tailored for it. References will also be given to other sources dealing with methods.

Second, the analysis of assessment data, if collected from multiple sources (administrators, Level 1 program recipients, service deliverers, stakeholders) by multiple or mixed methods (records, observations, interviews, questionnaires), is not an easy proposition. There are complexities in putting data together into a meaningful, coherent picture—reduction and interpretation may be difficult. Since the KIT cannot be all-inclusive about analyzing, collating, and portraying data, we concentrate on straightforward approaches for using methods and dealing with the jigsaw puzzle of needs data. There are utilitarian techniques and tricks of the trade for analyzing quantitative and qualitative data to define and prioritize discrepancies. Other insights into new and promising procedures will be provided.

Third, there is a difficulty that occurs in needs assessments when data are collected from multiple constituencies via different methods. (It is recommended that multiple methods and multiple groups routinely be used; see King & Jakuta, 2002.) Methods that might be implemented include in-person interviews with administrators; phone interviews with key informants (individuals representing groups who seem to know and understand issues); surveys with community members; examinations of records and databases; studies of social indicators; and so on. The results may totally agree (an ideal condition), may extensively agree, may partially agree, or may even be in total disagreement. The usage of multiple approaches to collecting data will be called *between methods*.

A *within-methods variation* is where different groups are exposed to subtle variations in an interview or a survey. It may not be possible to have the same wording and order of questions in surveys for highly varied constituencies. The phrasing for principals might not fit teachers. This was noted in a needs assessment conducted by Altschuld and others (1997) and by Lee et al. (2007a, 2007b). Could the ordering and subtle variations in questions produce results that cannot be compared and might affect the interpretation of results from groups? In some cases, this will add complexity to the needs assessment, especially in regard to needs-based decision making.

Fourth, where appropriate in the KIT, collaborative assessments across diverse organizations (in community services, health care delivery, and even business) will be suggested as a way to encourage cooperation for resolving problems. Yet it is recognized that each organization has its turf and characteristics and will tend to guard and control its space. We give practical advice for overcoming this barrier while recognizing that such forces might prevent meaningful, mutually beneficial cooperation.

Lastly, when an organization engages in a needs assessment, it will be dealing with new ideas and directions or uncovering weaknesses in how it is coping with a changing environment. The endeavor should foster discussion and reflection and demands that ways of doing things be examined. It should be open with input from multiple levels in an organization and from the constituencies it serves. Needs assessment should not be a top-down, "controlled" entity, which could breed stagnation and fear of growing and changing on the part of organizational staff. Some may perceive that they cannot voice opinions and will not do so. They may feel threatened or that the workplace does not permit the expression of views (jobs could be in jeopardy). Fear might lead to acquiescence, not commitment. *Alienation* is the word that captures the point. Some may quietly leave the organization.

Many organizations could, by not considering changed directions, die on the vine. This happened where dynamic and creative individuals left a national center and seldom continued any affiliation with it. The control had turned them off! Yet needs assessments must have administrative and leadership support that is sincere and freely given and that might even affect how higher or superordinate levels go about their business. Needs assessment falls in between leadership, management, and engendering a productive and exciting workspace. The examples throughout the KIT come from experience in a variety of such settings and demonstrate how issues were dealt with (successfully and unsuccessfully). Use our insights and benefit from the mistakes we have made.

❖ SOME NEEDS ASSESSMENT REFERENCES

The practice of needs assessment has been documented in books on theoretical aspects and ways to implement and conduct appropriate methods. In 1984, Witkin published a widely respected tome on the topic, notable for its extensive review and in-depth coverage of the literature. McKillip's (1987) text followed with subsequent efforts from the 1990s to the present day. The reader is referred to well-known books of Altschuld and Witkin (2000); Gupta (1999); Gupta, Sleezer, and Russ-Eft (2007); Kaufman, Rojas, and Mayer (1993); Reviere, Berkowitz, Carter, and Ferguson (1996); Soriano (1995); Wedman (2007); and Witkin and Altschuld (1995). Further back are the writings of Kaufman (1972, 1988) and Warheit, Bell, and Schwab (1979). Numerous articles can be located on specific needs assessments.

Highlights of the Chapter

You don't have to know all the concepts/ideas in this chapter. They are here to sensitize you to what needs assessment is and to enable you to do a better job of participating in or facilitating one. Here are some key points to remember as you move forward.

1. Individuals may not understand what needs are and what the needs assessment process entails, so some brief introduction about concepts is often required.

2. Needs are measured discrepancies between what is and what should be.

3. There is a *predisposition* to move to solution strategies before fully probing into needs—a tendency that has to be positively channeled.

4. Needs and solutions can be confused depending on how they are worded.

5. The "what should be" condition can be viewed in various ways (Tables 1.1 and 1.2).

6. There may be risks in not meeting needs.

7. Needs should be separated from wants.

8. Keep in mind Level 1, 2, and 3 needs with Level 1 being foremost.

9. Know the three phases of needs assessment and where the proposed effort is in terms of them.

10. The scope of an assessment (large, small) and the general nature of the needs area should be determined early in the process.

11. A collaborative needs assessment across organizations has high potential but may be difficult.

12. Include relevant constituencies in guiding the process and in providing information about needs. (Needs assessments are not *done* to a target group.)

13. Needs assessments are usually conducted by organizations as related to organizational change, development, and use of resources. They can be positive and political in nature.

14. Leadership support (not control) is important for a successful assessment study.

15. Needs assessment should lead to implementation of an action plan to resolve needs.

2

A Generic
Needs Assessment
Model and Steps

❖ INTRODUCTION

Let's expand the three-phase model for needs assessment. Its phases and steps take place in an organizational change and development context. Be sensitive to this and that politics may arise in such situations. The model appears to be linear with the three phases having 14 large numbered steps leading to the impression that assessment is a mechanical process. The steps prescribe exactly how to go about the process, and if followed, you will sail through it with a good breeze and no major whitecaps.

Nothing is further from the truth! We don't see this as limitation, however, for the steps provide guidance but are not a straitjacket. Needs assessment is partly technical and partly artistic and relies on the good sense of the needs assessment committee (NAC) and its facilitator. That stance is important given the issues involved in assessing needs—resource allocation, vested interests, multiple ways to go about assessment, and its effects on how organizations and people within them go about their business. How will the institution (agency, business) change to resolve the problems underlying needs? What is the commitment to do so given that change might not come easily? (Note how slowly the automobile industry in the United States is making its entry into fuel-efficient cars.) What about internal resistance when it comes to habitual ways of doing things and how resources are distributed?

The facilitator is a weaver of the tapestry of needs assessment and has to appreciate nuances to be successful. It takes skill, personality, experience, ability to adapt, willingness to live with ambiguity, and interaction with others particularly when conflict might arise. There are many twists and turns to the process; it is a negotiated process with compromises at every turn. It occurs in the social complexity of the organization or agency and the delicate intricacies found in unique settings. Balance must be achieved across constituencies with diverse perspectives of problems and their resolution. Self-interests and turf will come into play affecting the nature of the assessment even to the point of dominating it. Good luck!

Sometimes the process recycles back to earlier steps and retraces prior ground. Some steps may be out of order or overlap so that it is difficult to distinguish the phases from each other. Adding to the fun (this work is not dull!), a number of activities might be underway simultaneously. Expect these as a normal part of a needs assessment assignment. Be prepared for shifts in direction and obstacles. When previous steps are revisited, allow this to happen. Use simple summaries with the NAC and other groups to prevent consuming too much time. Find other ways (setting aside ideas for later scrutiny) to keep on task as much as feasible. Judging when or when not to press forward is important. Resolve disagreements through diplomacy and tact.

The twisting and turning nature makes it difficult to contract for an assessment. One way would be to contract for a subpart of the work, perhaps Phase I, and depending on what happens to contract for Phase II and/or 3 or specific pieces of work (conducting a survey, performing a causal analysis for the root causes of identified needs, etc.). This approach is what Wholey (1995) called the sequential purchase of information. By splitting what must be done, it is easier to develop budgets and estimates of time rather than guessing about the whole enterprise before starting; there are too many subtleties to anticipate in advance.

❖ THINKING ABOUT THE THREE-PHASE MODEL

While the three-phase, 14-step process covers the main elements of an assessment, there may be more steps (A. Goniprow & L. Ahmadi, personal communication, 2004). Needs assessment is evolving, and practice is changing. An altered version of the three phases is described later as "lagniappe" (something extra) to show how the process can be modified to fit special contexts.

The model may seem to be too much. Some assessments are for small entities or deal with not the most risk-oriented of situations (see Example 2.1). They are limited in scope or have few resources for their conduct that all steps cannot be done. In other cases, some steps may have been completed in other work by the organization or information related to them already exists, so only part of the 14-step process would be appropriate. Finances and time may necessitate that shortcuts be taken. Each needs assessment is specific to its setting and is planned accordingly.

Example 2.1

The World of Leisure and the Leisure World

Witkin (personal communication, 1994) described an interesting needs assessment that she conducted for the community in which she lived. It consisted of 300 modular homes with elderly and/or retired residents. What were their leisure, social, and educational needs; how could they be assessed; and what could the community do to improve the lives of its members? She convened a town hall meeting with over 50 attendees and had them do small- and large-group activities in a lively and somewhat fun atmosphere.

She guided a small planning group of community members (her NAC) in implementing the effort. They organized the meeting and arranged for and encouraged people to come. In the meeting, which lasted most of an afternoon, participants discussed what would be desirable in each of the areas for the community, what opportunities and activities currently existed, the nature of the discrepancies, and what actions could be taken for improvement. Voting and/or rank-ordering procedures were used to determine what was most important.

The session was serious yet casual, and the committee was able to get the management of the private community to provide refreshments and the community center for the activity. For a limited investment of time and money, a successful small needs assessment was conducted. Witkin capitalized on an almost hidden asset—the time and energies of a readily available senior population.

While the three-phase model covers all parts of assessing needs, it tolerates deviations from its prescriptions for each local circumstance. Pick and choose what is applicable and view it as a general guide to action. The model as originally proposed (Witkin, 1984) arose from intuition, not research. It was a practical way to proceed. In homage, that thinking was ahead of its time. Subsequent work by Altschuld and Witkin (2000) noted more complex aspects to the process, especially in relation to dimensions of the organization. The initial focus was on technical implementation with less attention to the organizational side. It has been argued that the prior views of needs assessment were somewhat shortsighted (see Altschuld, 2004).

❖   THE GENERIC MODEL

The three phases of the model are shown in Table 2.1. They are not mutually exclusive but overlap somewhat. The headings of Purpose, A Few Key Characteristics, and Decisions and cell entries give a sense of what the phases entail. This approach should be useful across health, education, community planning, social services, training, and development. Needs assessments generally go through the steps implicitly including the decisions made at the end of each phase.

❖   STEPS IN THE NEEDS ASSESSMENT PROCESS

In Table 2.2, the phases and key steps are presented. (Figure 2.1 is a simpler schematic useful for explaining needs assessment.) Keep in mind that Phase I is the foundation, the *sine qua non* condition of the needs assessment house.

Based on Phase I activities, it may not be necessary to do a full assessment or anything else at all. The need may not be there or of sufficient importance to warrant further action. Or in Phase I enough may have been learned about the gap to make a decision to resolve it and move directly to Phase III. Results from the first phase reduce work, time, and resources later in the needs assessment. Some of Phase I might recur in the other phases but in different ways and in greater depth.

❖   PHASE I: PREASSESSMENT—STEPS AND ACTIVITIES

How do we establish a focus for the needs assessment, and how does it begin? What do we know about the area of interest, or what information

Table 2.1 The Three-Phase Model of Needs Assessment

Phase	Purpose	A Few Key Characteristics	Decisions
Phase I Preassessment **Getting organized, and what do we know?**	Determine the focus of the needs assessment and get started	Formation of a group to guide the assessment Focusing in on main concerns Finding out what is already known	Do not go further; there is no need A more major needs assessment will have to be undertaken Move to Phase III, only if appropriate
Phase II Assessment **Do we need to know more, toward full understanding?**	Conduct a more in-depth examination of needs, if necessary Develop more understanding of needs at Levels 1, 2, and 3 Get a first sense of causes of needs and establish initial priorities	Implement needs assessment procedures such as surveys, focus group interviews, observations, analytic techniques, etc. Data collation and analysis Sort needs by levels	Understand needs in enough detail to move to Phase III Causes (at least some) of needs have been identified to guide either possible solution strategy development or selection
Phase III Postassessment **Moving toward actions based on needs**	Take action in regard to resolving the problem underlying the need	Causal analysis of needs Develop criteria for solution strategies Identify solution strategies via the literature, benchmarking, etc. Summative evaluation of needs assessment process Document the process for reuse at a later time	Decide to take action in regard to needs-based priorities Consider alternative action strategies and selection of same Build support in organization for implementation of action plans Evaluate the assessment

Table 2.2   The Needs Assessment Model (Phases and Key Steps)

Phase	Overarching Phase Descriptor	Key Steps
Phase I Preassessment	Focusing the needs assessment, and what do we know about possible needs?	1. Focusing the assessment 2. Forming an NAC 3. Learning as much as we can about preliminary "what should be" and "what is" conditions from *available* data sources 4. Moving to Phases II and/or III or stopping
Phase II Assessment	Do we need to know more, will we have to conduct a much more intensive data collection effort, and do we have ideas about what are the causes of needs?	5. Conducting a full assessment about "what should be" and "what is" conditions 6. Identifying discrepancies (Levels 1, 2, and 3) 7. Prioritizing discrepancies 8. Causally analyzing needs 9. Preliminary identification of solution criteria and possible solution strategies 10. Moving to Phase III
Phase III Postassessment	Are we ready to take action, and have we learned enough about the need to feel comfortable with our proposed actions?	11. Making final decisions to resolve needs and selecting solution strategies 12. Developing action plans for solution strategies, communicating plans, and building bases of support 13. Implementing and monitoring plans 14. Evaluating the overall needs assessment endeavor (document with an eye to revisit and reuse)

already exists and is easily obtained? Why are you being called in, or why are you being asked to get involved in the activity or to lead the effort? Assessments are undertaken due to changes in resources, a new source of funding demands that needs be identified and understood, issues emerging in the organization or group, and so forth.

Figure 2.1   What Is Needs Assessment?

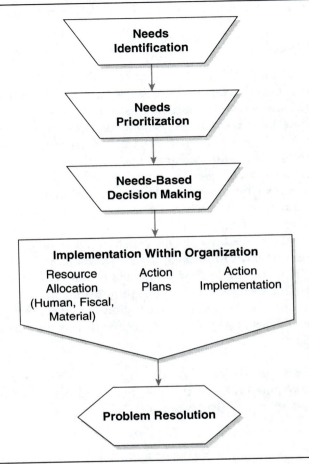

Let's assume a few administrators, a committee, or some stakeholders sense problems or needs to which attention must be given. The concern is vague, but there is a perspective that it should be looked at or there will be problems down the road that could become major and possibly intractable to resolve. It could be a feeling that not enough is being done, that the organization is not on the cutting edge and will fall behind if it doesn't deal with changes in the environment. Examples include the fact that the market share has been dropping, products are not appealing, competitors are being more successful, and so on. The group wants to change and improve but is not sure what to do. It has amorphous ideas about needs assessment, feels that it has to be organized to proceed, has limited prior participation in needs-related efforts, and requires help. So it is assigned to an individual who is internal to the organization or from outside but selected because of expertise or experience. A first task is to find out what the group really may need and what its understandings are.

Step 1 in Phase I

What do you do? That is the first step in Table 2.2. The process has to be *focused*. Given that needs can be vast and numerous, narrow the scope of the assessment by clarifying its purpose and specifying what will be done (see Altschuld & Eastmond, Book 2 of the KIT; and Eastmond, Witkin, & Burnham, 1987). Do reconnaissance as to why the group asked for help and what might be done. Additionally, note that needs assessments are used at times to defuse (co-opt) politically charged situations (groups that have not worked together previously, may be antagonistic to each other, or may push a predetermined administrative agenda, etc.).

Ask questions, read documents, meet with people individually or in small groups, and sort through ideas. If you are external, this time for interaction, meeting, review, and dialogue may not be reimbursed but is part of the cost of doing business prior to obtaining a contract for services. Informally chat with people to find out where they are, what is troubling them, and why they seek your help. Ask questions such as the following:

> What issue or problem is concerning you (or if the needs assessment is required for a proposal, have individuals describe what is being asked of the organization)?
>
> What do you know about it right now?
>
> What information has led you to this knowledge?
>
> Who is the group most affected (Level 1, 2, or 3) by the problem?
>
> What is your organization doing to work on this problem, and/or what kinds of services and programs are currently offered in this area?
>
> Would you consider new services should they be warranted?
>
> How committed to change is the organization given the nature of problems that a needs assessment might uncover?
>
> What would happen if the results led to needs and/or problems that were counter to current organizational thinking? Would the organization be able to handle this?
>
> Do you have ideas as to what is causing the problem?

What historical events led to the problem?

Are there different points of view about it? What individuals and/ or groups might hold them, and why do they hold them?

Is it really a high priority, and if so, why?

What are barriers that work against resolving this problem?

Has the organization looked at this issue before? If so, what was done, and what was learned about it?

Have any prior evaluations been done in this area?

Are personnel from the earlier effort available for discussion?

Are there previous data collection strategies that are accessible?

How did you learn about me as a possible facilitator of the needs assessment, and what do you think I can do for the organization?

Skim local documentation, records, and prior project materials with regard to the area of concern or a few relevant articles that can be rapidly located. How have other similar organizations facing this problem assessed needs? Ask if there is someone in the organization who can assist in conducting a mini literature review.

One useful tool for working with the organization early in the process was devised by Watkins and Guerra (2002). It is a brief scale consisting of needs assessment items (odd numbers) and evaluation ones (even numbers). Groups participating in the study of needs take the instrument and then see their scores on the two sets of items. The scores should be higher for needs-related ones than evaluation, but sometimes the distinction is not understood. Examining needs is oriented toward planning a program whereas evaluation assesses how well it is being implemented and the results it produces. You may be being asked to perform an evaluation, not to really look into needs, or the organization may want both activities.

The Watkins and Guerra (2002) instrument is a quick way to figure where the emphasis of the group is. (See Book 2 for a fuller description.) While it indicates a general direction, you have to delve more deeply to learn what is expected from the needs assessment. It could be about a part of the process such as causal analysis, action planning based on needs, serving as a focal point for local issues and concerns to arise, or some other aspect. Example 2.2 illustrates that many times professionals have only surface understandings about what needs assessment is and can do for them. So the facilitator is a teacher besides a technical expert and leader.

Example 2.2

Hey, You Don't Really Need a Needs Assessment!

A group of administrators in natural resources requested assistance in conducting a needs assessment. Preliminary discussions and exchanges quickly uncovered the fact that they already knew what the need was but simply did not understand what was causing it. Basically Phase I was completed as was much of Phase II. The best service that could be rendered was to provide a causal analysis (constructing a fault tree analysis, creating a fishbone diagram) or to lead a group where causes could be discussed and prioritized.

Aside from the needs versus evaluation survey, consider convening a small (five or so individuals) informal meeting of the group that wants to explore issues and perspectives. Take some of the list of initial questions from before and convert them into a framework for discussion or devise a short open-ended questionnaire about concerns and issues to use at the meeting to get participants to think about and write some of their thoughts. Having individuals jot down ideas and issues makes the discussion more tangible.

Include a cross-section of involved and interested parties. Needs assessors must guard against being insular, reflecting the views of a few. Appearance of same could affect the ultimate acceptance and utilization of results and raise suspicion about the intent of the needs assessment. Maintain evenhandedness while walking on this tightrope. This point is significant for results have to be openly communicated within the organization and to external constituencies. The enterprise should be characterized by meaningful involvement and participation of multiple stakeholders. Some insulation cannot be avoided, but too much impacts perceptions and ultimately may cause less-than-optimal buy-in to action plans.

There are many small-group techniques for focusing the investigation of needs. They are described in Books 2 and 5 in the KIT and explained in detail in other sources. They often employ forms and worksheets to get ideas of "what should be" and "what is" from group members, individually and collectively. The facilitator collates the information to guide the assessment. What is being created is an initial working document for the needs assessment. Examples 2.3 and 2.4 depict some early work carried out in actual assessments.

Example 2.3

Getting Those Initial Ideas

A suburban school district was growing rapidly with overcrowding problems in antiquated and inefficient buildings, particularly its one high school, which housed more than 3,000 students. Numerous additions had been made to the building, but they had not been done in a systematic manner. The high school was dysfunctional for the overcrowded circumstances.

District administrators saw this "need" as an opportunity to explore the possibility of new buildings with interesting and unique physical configurations, the outcomes the district should be striving to achieve, the ways in which the curriculum might be restructured, and how instruction might be delivered. A rare chance opened up for seriously assessing current and future needs.

To look at needs, the schools formed a needs assessment committee of teachers, administrators, and community members. They hired a well-known professor from the local university with expertise in community work to lead the effort. She had a reputation for fairness and willingness to look at all sides of an issue and guided the committee in the collection of existing data and information on current trends in education, the nature of what local and nearby communities in similar straits were doing, and societal factors occurring now or in the future that were pertinent. They synthesized what was learned into short (several pages), future-oriented scenarios, which were used in a series of small community group discussions. A list of community ideas and views on what the system should be accomplishing was derived from the group discussions.

The meetings were recorded via notes and audiotapes with summaries generated as to concerns, issues, and thoughts that had arisen. The summaries served as input for a needs assessment survey dealing with needs and possible solution strategies that was distributed to the households of the 35,000 individuals residing in the district. Eventually this led to the passage of a bond issue and a moderate restructuring of the educational system.

Example 2.4

The University Faculty

A small group of faculty and the chair of a large engineering department in a university became concerned about their curriculum and whether it reflected the emerging trends in the fast-moving field. One problem was the

(Continued)

(Continued)

extent to which current practice and new technologies and theory were contained in courses and how such entities should be delivered in class-rooms and laboratories. Were they up-to-date? Was instruction challenging and exciting? The field was evolving at breakneck speed. Remaining static was not realistic especially for the skills required by industry. Exploring these issues started out informally in discussions.

Eventually a formal committee was formed, and over a year it outlined the features, content, and instructional delivery strategy of main courses as compared to what was gleaned from the literature and syllabi of other universities. Later, the committee expanded to include several members from the university's College of Education who could enhance the value of the proceedings.

The information was analyzed and displayed in a table with courses as the rows and columns for current features (the "what is" dimension) and for best practices (the "what should be") as derived from the committee's research. Comparisons were made looking for discrepancies and potential next steps. The committee made tentative decisions as to what was to be kept or discarded and what were the most likely targets for change or addition to the curriculum. In effect, the committee had done the preassessment phase. It proceeded to more widespread dialogue in the department and developed plans for a partial curriculum revision (incorporating ideas from the dialogue). The effort led to a proposal seeking external funds for revision of the curriculum revision. The committee moved from Phase I directly into Phase III without any additional data collection.

Example 2.4 is similar to an idea proposed by Kaufman, Stakenas, Wagner, and Mayer in 1981. They suggested that we look at "what is" and "what should be" for organizational inputs, processes, outputs, and outcomes as well as societal outcomes, with the thought that these entities are linked together in a chain. Based upon discrepancies in the five components, decide what should be maintained and/or changed and what new endeavors might be undertaken.

Examples 2.3 and 2.4 demonstrate the value of preassessment and how it led to further data collection (2.3) or directly facilitated the development of action plans (2.4). Step 1 in Phase I helps facilitators (especially if external) get a sense of why their services were requested and how their skills might benefit the enterprise. In both examples, the facilitators were involved early in the deliberations, which is important for understanding the groups and what was behind their unease. Coming in later would not have worked so well.

When sought as a facilitator, question why you were asked to be there. Are all sources of information available and accessible? Are there sacred cows that will make the job more difficult? Is there sincere commitment to change on the part of the organization? Are individuals willing to change and use their energies for betterment? Is the situation cooperative or so confrontational that nothing will be accomplished? Analyze context and actors, and if there are going to be problems, think about ways to eliminate them or lessen their impact. Be upbeat, be persistent, and recognize that as time passes, confrontation and conflict frequently ebb.

Furthermore, be aware that needs assessments might be due to that little *p* word (politics). Is it being done in response to a political bone of contention? Might it be for the purpose of deflecting attention from a critical issue or to ease pressure among groups that do not like each other or work together? Could the statement "Yes, we are in the process of examining the issue for action at a later date" be a stand-in for diverting attention away from a problem or defusing what might be a source of tension? This might be the co-opting strategy noted earlier; the reason for the assessment is that interest in the problem and energy will dissipate with psychological distance and the passage of time. *So let's get rid of the issue by doing a needs assessment!*

The assessment is not for the purpose traditionally assigned to it. Political disagreements, however, can be the impetus for seeing if a need exists. The *caveat emptor* for the facilitator is that the "whys" may not be what you think they are. Ascertain motives and see if the needs assessment will result in growth and movement forward, even if limited. Can some good result, or can attitudes and perspectives be changed to promote a more positive atmosphere? If it is too political and change will not occur and if you are external to the situation, politely withdraw. Funding is lost, but dignity is preserved. If you are internal, the option to withdraw may not be there. A way to salvage the situation whether you are internal or external would be by implementing Step 2 in Phase I.

Before leaving Step 1, in Examples 2.3 and 2.4 enthusiasm was there with a high probability of something worthwhile happening. Many needs assessments are like these. There were major problems that required attention, and a sincere effort was going to be made to learn about and resolve them. This is when the work is exciting for the organization, facilitator, and NAC.

Step 2 in Phase I

Needs assessments require the guidance and involvement of committees. *Step 2 in Phase I* specifies an NAC to guide the effort. It is an engaged, enthusiastic working group—invaluable for the collection of data, their analysis, and other steps in the needs assessment. The facilitator should observe who in the organization or among its stakeholders is or is not involved in deliberations. Absence of a group or set of individuals might tip off political agendas, ones that are subtle and covert. Gently and tactfully ask questions about the inclusion of others in the process. See if it would be possible and judicious to expand the NAC. Use questions such as those that follow to feel out the political and power dimensions:

What groups or individuals might have a key interest in the needs assessment and eventual programs and activities that might result from it?

Are there standing committees or groups that have been included before and should remain connected to it?

Are there individuals or groups who were not involved but should be now?

Would there be conflicts if we formed an NAC across the following groups?

Are there political agendas that might come up that would negatively affect this needs assessment?

What individuals would make positive contributions to the NAC?

How will decisions be made in the organization(s) about the results of this endeavor?

Should we be working collaboratively with other agencies and/or institutions?

Are there individuals who, although not in formal positions of authority, are informal power brokers behind the scenes and should be included?

The NAC should consist of representatives of key stake-holding constituencies that might be affected by new programs or have vested interests in the outcomes of the study. Select them thoughtfully as they should be aware of the nuances of the groups from which they come. Ideally, they should be a part of how decisions are made in their groups, have access to decision makers, or be able to influence decisions. If they have experience working in collaborative endeavors, enjoy and appreciate diversity, and know when to compromise and/or to take a position, that would be a plus, and they would make excellent NAC members.

The NAC is situated as Step 2 instead of Step 1. An NAC is essential to the success of the entire needs assessment process, but it is better placed as the second step after reconnaissance is completed. Choose group members wisely and well. How large should the group be? Is it more appropriate to have a small group (under 10) that can more readily arrive at consensus or a larger one (20–25) that affords more resources (working subgroups) for assessment tasks and has more points of view? Size comes with a cost. Twenty-five people (instead of 8–10) require more time and coordination of the facilitator. It will not be as easy to reach consensus of the larger group. Subgroups can be productive but also uneven. How to proceed rests upon the facilitator's understanding of the internal relationships of the organization, past work with groups of different sizes, and the amount of contention in the needs assessment.

Step 3 in Phase I

Now that an NAC has been formed, the assessment has been narrowed a bit, and there is an inkling of the "what should be" and the underlying problem(s) or area(s) of concern. Next the process moves to *Step 3 in Phase I, finding out more about the "what should be" and "what is" conditions and expanding understanding of them.* (Remember the first phase is to get organized and determine what knowledge already exists.) Collect as much existing information as possible. It would be ill advised at this time to obtain information other than what is available and accessible. Producing new data is costly, unique instruments may have to be developed or found, and elongated periods for collection might be necessary. Such activities can tire out the NAC and dampen enthusiasm, and new data may not yield enough novel understandings of the problem to warrant the costs. What is available is cheaper and may be sufficient.

Depending on the nature of the needs area, here is where a larger NAC may be an asset. Divide it into subgroups with each locating specific sets of data, reports, resources that the organization has, and other materials. Some NAC members will know about existing sources. They may have data skills and have been in similar situations before. Choices for NAC membership should be made deliberately for the members usually have a profound (positive or negative) influence on the needs assessment.

Where does the information come from? First, consult with your local community (United Way, regional planning groups, and the like), school system, or chamber of commerce or with librarians who are nearby (see Example 2.5). The latter are very knowledgeable about

Example 2.5

How a Librarian Helps the Needs Assessment Process

Think about the development of this KIT as a form of needs assessment. The NAC (i.e., the authors) knew a lot about the theory, process, and procedures of needs assessment—a kind of "what is" status. Some of them have written about the field for years and are quite familiar with "what should be," but it is a kind of static (not dynamic) "what should be." What is happening now? How is the practice changing? What new techniques and approaches are appearing?

In terms of preassessment, some of the authors have attended professional meetings on the topic; they have conducted their own searches or sought the help of a librarian to obtain more up-to-date information. By this means, new ideas such as the survey for determining whether evaluation or needs assessment is being asked for, the idea of asset assessment, subtleties in the use of existing data, and others have been added to the text.

where and how to look and may graciously make time to assist in the search process. They may be aware of studies that have been done by charitable groups, businesses, state agencies, and other entities.

Second, the organization itself may have done evaluations and needs assessments in the past, or it may regularly collect data that would be useful for the present investigation in the form of record-keeping strategies or a management information system (MIS). Many organizations have developed databases and spreadsheets and have extensive information about their clientele (students, clients, patients, consumers, etc.) and the programs and products they offer. There are internal personnel who have responsibility for and skills in extracting information from the bases or aligning them with external databases. They may be willing to perform some analyses for the assessment, or if there is sufficient support, they may be assigned to assist the venture. Seeking such help must be done in a positive way instead of as a top-down directive. Enlist this assistance so data analyzers feel integral to an important and useful task. It might be judicious to include a person with good data skills on the NAC.

Databases should be accessed only for collated analysis purposes with the privacy of individuals never to be violated. Lastly, be aware of what is or is not in the database and what governs entries to it. Since most of these data are quantitative, an admonition from basic statistics comes to mind and is paraphrased as "Numbers tell you everything, and numbers tell you nothing." (For problems in information from such sources see Altschuld & Witkin, 2000.)

How much information is enough, and from how many sources should it be obtained? The size and scope of the needs assessment, the underlying problem being investigated, and the risks (consequences) associated with taking or not taking action influence how much information is needed. In some health-related areas (diabetes, heart disease, SARS, HIV/AIDS) and some social concerns (driving under the influence, recidivism, returning pedophiles and sex offenders to the community and the possibility of their resuming negative behaviors), risk factors are serious, and a lot of information is desirable. In others (recreational needs of a small retirement community, needs of a small faculty group in a college), the demand is not so great.

The number of sources is relative. If the data overlap to a high extent, not much is needed from multiple sources and constituencies. Other times, it might be politically wise to touch many bases when obtaining data. The NAC and its facilitator use judgment in deciding how to use its fiscal, people, and time resources. One rule is to stop if what you already have is becoming repetitious. Another observation is that with multiple sources it becomes harder to synthesize them into a meaningful guide for decision making.

Step 4 in Phase I

Step 4 in Phase I deals with rendering knowledge into an integrated whole that helps the NAC arrive at understanding and making intelligent choices as to what should be done next. Three concepts are in play here. First is *Synthesizing Data.* The NAC may have qualitative and quantitative data from disparate sources and methods—records, prior studies, spreadsheets, databases, social indicators compiled by community agencies, interviews, and so forth. The information might or might not fit together. The NAC has to weigh the quality of each source to arrive at its decisions and interpret information that agrees or disagrees or is quite different in content. Synthesis may not be a simple task (see Chapter 5 and Book 4).

The second concept is *Rendering Data.* Use the KISS principle, Keep It Short and Simple. How many of us have sat through meetings that went on without end, ones in which a data analyst went through every nuance of analysis even though all of that was less than incisive, relevant, and needed for decisions? What happens to thought processes when attention has worn thin and we no longer can absorb the key and most important information? If the focus is too heavy on statistically oriented results and outcomes, it may come at the expense of practical or substantive meaning. Statistical significance may be obtained with large samples for relatively small effect sizes, thus complicating decision-making processes. Being succinct and direct helps groups agree on the next steps in the needs assessment and to have a successful meeting. If the collation process isn't thoughtful, gestalt can be lost as to what the meeting is to accomplish and where it is going. It is necessary to know how the data were analyzed and the validity of that analysis, but every detail might not be vital, and keep in mind that there will be results from many different methods from which meaning must be constructed. Data must be in a usable format and structure to guide the NAC.

Therefore, it is recommended that the facilitator or a segment of the NAC produce synopses of each source with brief explanations of how the data were analyzed and main findings. Then a snapshot of where the data agree and where they do not should guide discussions and deliberations of the NAC.

The last concept is *Meaningfulness.* Technically successful needs assessments can fail in terms of utility unless they have been translated into the vernacular of decision-making groups. An example of what the need means to a person or group would be helpful in putting a human face on an issue.

The synopses and compiled results are distributed to the NAC with members being asked to read them prior to a decision-making meeting. Now we have moved to how this amalgam of information will guide us in making needs-based decisions. An illustration of what can happen when a large amount of data is obtained by different methods is shown in Example 2.6. One principle here is that it is wise to think through in advance multiple methods, data integration, and portrayal for decision-making purposes.

Example 2.6

Sometimes It's Difficult to Fit Those Data Together

A public health needs assessment conducted in Canada was interesting. A large NAC and many of its members were involved in subparts of the study. That study was remarkable in that multiple constituent groups provided information and multiple methods, qualitative and quantitative, were employed. Data at an amazing level of depth came from records, surveys, and individual and focus group interviews. While each aspect of the study was conducted with a high level of skill, it proved difficult to pull together the complex set of information that emerged.

At the next meeting, highlights of the results are reviewed, and the NAC engages in a decision-oriented discussion. Questions helpful in this context are:

What are your impressions of the data that have been collected?

Are there any major areas of data or information that you feel are missing? If so, what are they, and do you know where they might be located?

Are there other methods of data collection that should be considered (surveys, focus group interviews, community interviews and forums, tests)?

Are you comfortable with what is now known about the need(s)?

What groups and how many people are affected by these needs?

In general, how important do the needs seem?

What might it take to resolve some of these problems?

Are there other organizations or agencies that have faced the same or related problems?

Do we know about how they identified their needs and how they have resolved them?

Do we have a clear view of needs at Level 1, recipients; Level 2, service providers; and Level 3, the system that supports Levels 1 and 2?

What might be causing the needs at the three levels?

Is there enough understanding of needs, their importance, and the risks involved in them to make decisions on how to proceed?

How should we move forward in terms of the next phases of needs assessment (the facilitator quickly summarizes options for the NAC)?

Many of the questions are designed with other phases in mind. If more existing information is desired, then postpone decisions until it is collected and added to the mix, or if the group wants to move into Phase II, do so. If the NAC wants to dig into causality for any of the three levels or to know more about risk factors before dealing with criteria for priorities or solutions, go to the appropriate step in Phase II.

The questions that deal with other organizations encountering similar needs and resolving such problems are tied into action planning, Phase III. They deal with benchmarking, seeking out organizations that have probed into similar needs (their decisions and what worked in their settings). Overall the NAC will decide to move to Phase II or III or go no further depending on what was learned in preassessment.

❖ PHASE II: ASSESSMENT

If it is necessary to conduct a full needs assessment (*Phase II, Step 5*), the first consideration will be what is known about the "what should be" and "what is" conditions of Level 1 (and of Levels 2 and 3, *Step 6*). What would be most useful to collect at this time guides Phase II work. Example 2.7 is another way to conduct the three-phase model especially for large, major investigations of needs.

Example 2.7

An Alteration to the Model, a Little Something Extra, or "Lagniappe"

An area within the U.S. Department of Education decided to conduct a nationwide needs assessment employing the three-phase model by pilot testing the procedures and general strategy in four states before going to national scale. From the pilot test it was found that it may be better to conduct all three phases first for Level 1 before dealing with Levels 2 and 3. While information pertinent to the needs of the latter levels arises normally in the Level 1 assessment, it would be catalogued for use only after all facets of Level 1 needs were clarified. It is probable that the subsequent assessments for Levels 2 and 3 would be somewhat easier given what had already been learned about the prime needs.

Do we require more information about the gap between "what should be" and "what is"? Would it be desirable to learn about what subgroups are or will be affected? Is the need short- or long-term? Is it slight or severe? How amenable is it to resolution? What, amongst its features, provides the most guidance for selecting a solution strategy? What do we know about the risks in meeting the need or simply letting things stay the same (the counterfactual state)? What are the critical causal factors underlying a need?

The NAC naturally flows into Phase II. The data array from the end of Phase I helps the committee pinpoint what to do. It is helpful here if the facilitator has experience with the needs assessment process and methodology. Lay out possible choices for obtaining in-depth data and information. Should focus group interviews, nominal group techniques, individual interviews, Delphi surveys, or other techniques be used? Do we need quantitative data from epidemiological analyses, surveys, and so forth? Most assessments routinely use three types of methods for collecting data—archival sources (more relevant to Phase I), communication strategies (interactive and noninteractive), and analytical approaches. Often techniques from the categories are used in conjunction with each other. Table 2.3 has an overview of methods.

Table 2.3   An Overview of Needs Assessment Methods

Data Type	Comments/Description	Information Generated
ARCHIVAL Records/logs Social indicators Demographic data Census data Epidemiological studies Rates under treatment Test data Information derived from databases Other similar existing sources	Data do not have to be created but exist usually in routinely maintained databases or records The needs assessor, in some instances, may be able to initiate new record-keeping systems for collecting data Existing data may not exactly match the intent of the needs in question	Mostly quantitative data about the current ("what is") status of target groups Data may lead to understandings about causal or contributing factors of needs Some databases or records might include comments and notes, necessitating qualitative analyses and interpretation
COMMUNICATIVE—NONINTERACTIVE Written questionnaires Critical incident technique Mailed Delphi surveys Web-based surveys Observations	These methods rely primarily on structured instruments or forms Surveys will employ scaled questions Usually a few open-ended questions will be included in questionnaires Observations may either follow detailed protocols or permit more freedom in describing the phenomenon under consideration	While some of the data obtained can be very quantitative in nature, remember they often come from the values, judgments, and opinions of those providing responses and perspectives

(Continued)

Table 2.3 (Continued)

Data Type	Comments/Description	Information Generated
COMMUNICATIVE—INTERACTIVE Public hearings Community group forums Nominal group techniques Focus group interviews (FGIs) Cyber or virtual FGIs Interviews Key informant interviews DACUM process Scenario discussions	Aside from key informant interviews these procedures involve the use of small or large groups with varying degrees of interaction Group leadership is especially critical to the success of the procedures and the results produced	Highly qualitative data that will have to be summarized into themes and reoccurring concepts Data will be about group perceptions, opinions, judgments, and values Information might deal with consensus on goals, courses of action, causes, priorities, and the like
ANALYTIC Fishbone diagrams Cause and consequence analysis Quality function deployment Fault tree analysis Success mapping Task analysis Risk assessment Trend analysis Cross-impact analysis Force field analysis	Processes done by groups to examine solution strategies, causes or risks associated with needs, and/or ways to resolve them Results might be summarized in graphs or diagrams emanating from the analytic process	Highlighted problems that might lead to the failure of a solution strategy Guidance in choosing a resolution for a need that would have a high likelihood of succeeding With other information from the needs assessment process, makes for a fuller (more comprehensive) understanding of the need

Source: Adapted from *Planning and Conducting Needs Assessments: A Practical Guide,* by B. R. Witkin and J. W. Altschuld, 1995, Thousand Oaks, CA: Sage. Adapted with permission.

Note: Other versions of this type of table could be devised by needs assessors as befit their local situations. They are encouraged to adapt tables like this for local use.

Commonly employed methods are discussed in Book 3 of the KIT. Some guidelines for choosing what to use are as follows:

- Consider the NAC, the constituencies it represents, and what key staff and administrators perceive as creditable sources of data and information (sound out a few individuals to get a sense of this).

- How much budget is allotted for data collection?

- Would more data be worth the cost, or would it be better to look at causes of needs and so on?

- Be parsimonious in the choice of methods and data to be collected.

- Consider the skills needed for analyzing and summarizing data.

- How much data is to be collected, and from what size sample should it be obtained?

- If other assessments have been found, look at their methods and how the data were analyzed and presented.

- Seek existing instruments, and if they don't exactly fit, see if they can be modified (developing new instruments and data collection procedures is costly).

- Overall, how will new data enhance knowledge of discrepancies and what is causing them, and what might occur if we do or do not deal with identified needs?

From a perusal of the methods in the table, it should be apparent that most of the communicative and analytic strategies fit Phases II and III.

Steps 6, 7, and 8 of Phase I are for defining and prioritizing discrepancies and determining what causes them. For *Step 6*, analyze and show the data in a way that will enable the NAC and others to see the chain of logic that is underlying your thinking. One simple organizing schema is shown in Table 2.4. Certainly, almost all of the data collection mechanisms will result in much more detailed qualitative and quantitative findings than summarized in the table. There will be reams of material produced. These should be studied by the NAC, but remember that sheer volume may overwhelm the committee. The table is a simple mechanism to aid the decision-making process. The last column allows the committee to consider other information that has come up during the needs assessment.

Table 2.4 One Format for Portraying Overall Needs Assessment Discrepancy Data

Area of Focus	Information Collected	"What Should Be" State	"What Is" State	Nature of Discrepancy	Other Comments
Area 1	Surveys and focus group interviews with physicians	Holding steady or decreasing rate of lung cancer among women	Recent and noticeably increasing incidence of this cancer	Data and brief look at literature indicate that only part of rise is due to smoking	Data and interviews suggest that the rate will continue to rise and the discrepancy will increase
Area 2	——	——	——	——	——
Area n	——	——	——	——	——

The next concern is to prioritize findings (*Step 7*) so that resources can be targeted to the highest need areas—easier said than done. In conducting workshops on this topic, Altschuld, Cullen, & Witkin (1996) found that even those who supposedly knew about needs assessment could not describe systematic procedures for prioritizing needs. Since resources are allocated against priorities, there should be a well-defined and defensible procedure for doing this.

There are numerous approaches for setting priorities with a well-known one being that of Sork (1998). Sork posited that there were five criteria dealing with *importance* (number of people affected by the need, size of the discrepancy, and others) and three for *feasibility* (cost, organizational commitment, degree to which an education intervention will fix the problem). The last criterion may seem odd, but solutions are delivered by adult service providers, and hence this criterion would be suitable for almost all solution strategies. Altschuld and Witkin (2000) added risk factors to Sork's list. (In Chapter 1, there was a brief treatment of risk.)

Risks are internal to the organization (morale, internal politics) or external (market share, public relations, etc.). When a needs assessment is about a major area of concern and its resolution involves shifting resources, a formal prioritizing process including risks is mandatory to withstand public scrutiny. If need is not as critical, try simple procedures such as voting or rank-ordering work.

Step 8, determining what causes a need, has come up previously in the needs assessment. Some ideas about causality and solutions appear even though they have not been formally examined. They pop up in

Phases I and II. (This is why the last column in Table 2.4 was included.) The facilitator keeps track of them just for this moment. In smaller efforts all that might be required is an NAC discussion of causal factors and which among them are most important and likely. If there are many possible causes of a problem, usually only a small subset are causing it.

Formal causal analysis techniques include fault tree analysis (FTA), fishboning, cause consequence analysis, and others. In larger assessments with more serious consequences, they should be used. Some are complicated and require an investment of time and effort, but if the need is especially important, use them. An interesting feature of FTA is that causal factors are separated into those under control of the organization and ones that it is unable to control or change. With the cause of a need understood, it may be advantageous to go back to Step 7 and rethink prioritization. Should a lesser need with a better chance of resolution be favored over a higher one that is less likely to be resolved? The NAC should briefly review what was done before and be willing to shift priorities if that seems advantageous.

Why is *Step 9* in this phase? Determining a solution strategy and how to implement it takes place in Phase III, so why is it here? Throughout the previous eight steps needs have been identified and prioritized, but the NAC probably has gone beyond these activities. It has a sense of causes and what might be required to solve problems. Inklings of what a solution might look like and criteria for solution strategies have been thought about and suggested. These are useful, so capitalize and build upon them.

Step 10 is making decisions for Phase III. The final meeting of the NAC in Phase II is facilitated by having slightly more elegant versions of tables along the lines of Table 2.4 including such things as prioritized needs, how they were prioritized, possible or probable causes, potential criteria for solutions, and some solution strategies. Such materials are reviewed to guide future activities. Everyone should be on the same page at this point. In the 10 previous steps, the forms, summaries, and specialized tables are the audit trail of what the NAC has accomplished—the official record of the needs assessment. They are a means of communicating results of the process to the staff and administration of the organization and others. Communication with all groups should be a regular happening as the NAC hits decision points and as key information and findings are generated. Schedule the communication when it would be most propitious.

❖   PHASE III: POSTASSESSMENT

It is wise to add a few new members to the NAC. How can this be done without disrupting things? Since the NAC has been working together for a long period, relationships are there, people know each other, and work is getting done—what's the rationale for doing something that could upset the applecart? The needs assessment is moving toward an action plan, and it is beneficial to expand with those who know how things get done. Their insights for action planning are invaluable for Phase III. Raise this with the NAC, and if it agrees, include several individuals using the criteria for NAC membership specified earlier. This may not be difficult— some members have left, or others may be amenable to leaving or being replaced. This should be discussed tactfully and openly.

Step 11 is completed at the end of Phase II or as the first one in Phase III and has been placed in Phase III to cement the phases together. *Step 12* is based upon what we have from Phase II (identified/prioritized needs, causal analyses of them, a partial list of ideas and specifications, and criteria useful for designing, selecting, and/or adapting a solution strategy).

Reviewing the literature for alternative solutions, benchmarking, and brainstorming are ways in which to approach this step. More sophisticated but complicated methods would be QFD (quality function deployment from manufacturing) and MAUT (multi-attribute utility theory or its derivatives). In 2000, Altschuld and Witkin proposed a table (see Chapter 5) for comparing solution strategies selected from the literature or from benchmarking with other organizations. Benchmarking requires resources for visiting sites and observing what their solutions are and how they operate. This shows what can come up in needs assessment and where funds might not have been included in original budgets.

But there is more to Step 12. Carefully choosing a solution strategy against a variety of factors is a prerequisite for action planning (activities, timelines, responsibilities, resources, evaluation of outcomes, etc.). Juxtapose that plan against the forces in the organization that are supportive or in opposition. Looking at Figure 2.2, the goal would be to devise ways to ameliorate forces against and strengthen those in favor of the new direction.

When agreement is reached, the organization begins to initiate the new course, monitor its development and implementation, and see what is being achieved. At last, success (*Step 13*)! The needs assessment is over. The process has gone from its beginning (let's look at needs) to an action plan that has been accepted and is underway. At last, it's over—or is it that "it ain't over till it's over" (attributed to Yogi Berra, a famous American baseball player)?

How well did it work? What was learned from engaging in the process? What will happen in a few years when we reassess needs? Needs change and evolve with time. *Step 14* reinforces the idea that the needs assessment itself should be evaluated. How did we get to this

Figure 2.2 Force Field Analysis of Organizational Factors That Could Affect the Success or Failure of a Solution Strategy

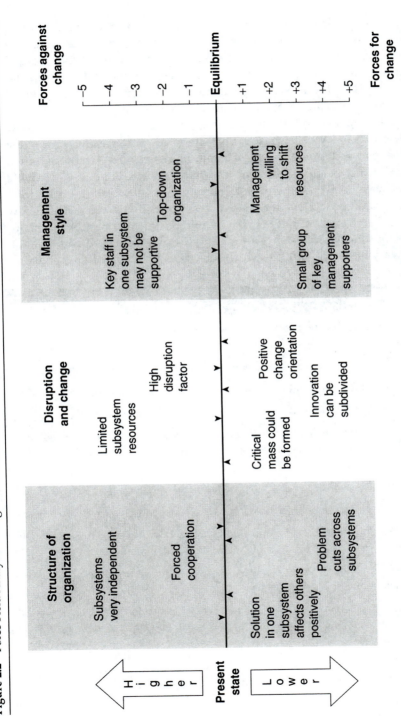

Source: From *Needs Assessment to Action: Transforming Needs Into Solution Strategies,* by J. W. Altschuld and B. Witkin, 2000, Thousand Oaks, CA: Sage. Used with permission.

point, and what can be passed along for the next time needs will be assessed? Were there needs that were not attended to but that now reemerge? Are there instruments that might be reused? What worked well, and what would not be recommended for subsequent assessments?

Step 14 is the reason why documentation of the process and an audit trail are so important. They are the basis for organizational history and learning. Beyond documentation, conduct a focus group interview with the NAC where the quality, strengths, and weaknesses of the endeavor are discussed and analyzed. Its results are put into the final record of the needs assessment. In Chapter 6 and Book 5, we provide some ways in which the evaluation might be conducted. Lastly don't lose sight of the fact that the needs assessment might have revealed how a solution strategy might fail. This would be critical input for the evaluation of the solution strategy—identifying key formative and summative variables and points at which the assessments should be made.

Highlights of the Chapter

1. Recognize that the needs assessment process is molded to fit the setting and situation.

2. It is important to understand how the assessment got started and its focus.

3. The first few meetings may have somewhat of an educational flavor.

4. Make good choices for NAC membership to enhance its success.

5. Ensure that the NAC is clear about the purpose of the needs assessment, where it is in the process (Phase I, II, or III), and which of the three levels is being stressed.

6. Emphasis on Phase I is warranted since all activity stems from it.

7. At the end of Phase I, obtain consensus on the decision regarding next steps.

8. Throughout the process, summaries of data and what has taken place help the NAC. They are also valuable for evaluation and communication purposes.

9. NAC membership may change somewhat in Phase III as the needs assessment moves into action plans.

10. Communication about the process and its evaluation are often neglected. Provisions should be made in needs assessment budgets for attending to them.

3

Phase I: Preassessment

❖ INTRODUCTION

The "nitty-gritty" details of this phase are not emphasized to a great degree; rather the idea is to give a basic understanding of how to carry out main activities (often in the form of lists). Since needs assessments must be attuned to local politics and personalities, the focus of the assessment, available resources, and other factors, guidelines are appropriate. The three phases are flexible and modified to fit small or large organizations (government agencies, businesses, and state and national programs). Phase I is about establishing a clear direction for what potentially could be accomplished by the effort.

Due to high variability, it is complicated to plan needs assessments and budget for costs, personnel, and other aspects of the work. In 1987, Eastmond, Witkin, and Burnham suggested an intensive orientation activity that provides the facilitator and/or the needs assessment committee (NAC) with a better understanding of what is required and how to determine assignments, time required, and so on. (That approach has mutated into the cultural audit in Book 2 of the KIT.)

Assessments might, from inception, be thought of in a "chunked" fashion, which entails focusing on discrete and smaller pieces and contracting for more activity as warranted by the progress made. For example, in Phase I, assume that very preliminary (exchange of ideas) discussions have taken place with a few interested parties (administrators, key personnel, concerned individuals), and some initial information and data are available and have been perused. Going further, a number of meetings are scheduled with persons who might become potential NAC members to sort out possibilities for Phase I. This is a "chunk" of work.

If you are an external facilitator, consider the costs for meetings, materials to be prepared for them, summaries to be generated, refreshments and support, and other conditions that lead to success. Try to build in a few of the costs incurred in earlier interactions if you are able. In most instances that time will have been gratis with little or no remuneration, typical for this type of work! If you are internal and were assigned to the facilitator role or "volunteered" for it, some expenses have already been taken into account by the organization. In any case, the concerns for meetings are the same as above, and the chunking principle still applies.

Once one piece of the needs assessment is completed and there are indications that more steps and actions are necessary, they too could be divided into smaller, more manageable segments of work. This is similar to the sequential purchase of information mentioned in the prior chapter. A couple of other things are important before moving to the steps in Phase I.

First, is external or internal important? The internal facilitator has the advantage of knowing the organization, its personnel, and how it functions. The external individual tends to be more objective and not to represent any vested organizational interests. All organizations will have to think about internal or external facilitation of the process. While it is cheaper to utilize internal personnel for leadership, in the long run it might be "pennywise but pound foolish" (see Example 3.1).

Example 3.1

Don't Be Pennywise but Pound Foolish!

A public service organization, which receives support from state and federal sources, was undergoing cutbacks in funding. At the same time it was subject to rapidly changing demands with some of its services having lost their relevance. To deal with this the organization decided to conduct regional and, in some instances, countywide needs assessments via community group forums (town meetings). It sought advice on how these should be facilitated and what persons would be best to lead them. The organization was leaning toward internal regional and local personnel to reduce costs. It asked a needs assessment specialist to review its proposed approach. The advice was to have a smaller number of sessions led by external individuals with the assistance and guidance of internal agency personnel.

Although the organization and internal personnel had the best of intentions, bias would probably have crept into the process. No matter how much they may try to not favor a particular viewpoint, internal staff may be unable to adopt the neutral stance necessary for facilitation. They bring historical baggage with them. In a subtle way, they could exude a slant on issues that may be obvious to participants in group sessions. The validity of results could be affected and called into question. In general, external facilitators will not favor any specific position—they are there to help a group open up and uncover its perceptions and feelings. The external facilitator may not have intimate knowledge of the situation and could be aided via the assistance of an internal person, but the trade-off in neutrality is too great to make the case for being pennywise by having internal individuals conduct the meetings.

Second, how much should be charged for services? Budgeting is fraught with problems arising from the politics of the situation, the harmony or disharmony of working relationships in the organization, and the many changes in direction that occur in needs assessments. What to charge is never easy to answer. A colleague (B. R. Worthen, personal communications over years) who had a very successful academic and consulting career mentioned a novel way to bill for services. For short-term jobs (a week or less) a higher daily rate deals with some of the unpaid, up-front work and the intensity that short-term tasks require. It is scaled down for a prolonged engagement. One advantage of this strategy is that it may encourage organizations to do a better, in-depth assessment with long-term expert advice shaping the process.

❖ PROCEDURES FOR PHASE I: PREASSESSMENT

Step 1: Focusing the Needs Assessment

Focusing activities are shown in Figure 3.1; use the figure to orient groups to the initial dimensions of a needs assessment. Details are below.

1a. Preliminary Scoping of the Situation

Ask questions (see Chapters 1 and 2) in your first meetings with those who requested your services. See if there are individuals you could informally interview about their perspectives, what the issues are, where the organization currently is, what kinds of problems it

Figure 3.1 Step 1: Focusing the Needs Assessment

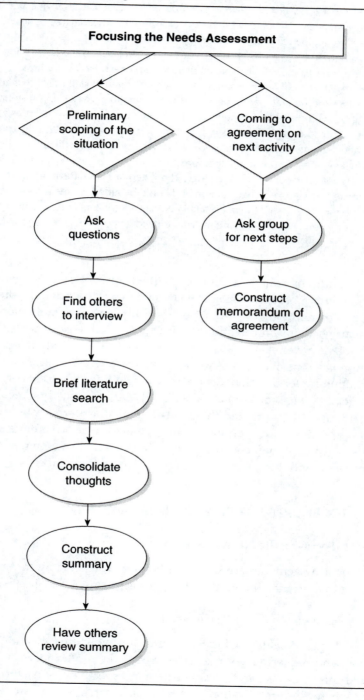

might run into in the future, and so on. (Make sure that you maintain the confidentiality of responses.)

Be alert for political issues and concerns; try to get a feel for how the organization ticks and how open or closed it might be. (Are some individuals or groups being excluded? Do people freely voice their opinions even when negative about something? Do they appear cautious, guarded, or even afraid and thus to be holding back? If so and you are external, consider gracefully bowing out—you don't need the headaches. If you are internal, think about focusing on a smaller part of the issue and where you can do some good.)

Conduct a quick, brief Web-based literature search on the topic(s) of interest or on other organizations that have recently undergone experiences or changes similar to this one. Read or skim a few articles.

Consolidate the concerns that arise, what seems to be the nature of the problem(s), what might be apparent about the "what should be" and "what is" states, the individuals and groups that make up the three levels, and other appropriate aspects. Keep the summary short and to the point—5–10 pages, a few tables, highlighted recommendations, and items for discussion. Consider such things as the following:

- What is the scope and size of the area(s) or topic(s) of interest?

- Would it be of value to divide the area(s) or topic(s) into sub-clusters or themes?

- Would it be useful to collect more information?

- Would the collection of new data be warranted?

- Will going to a full set of Phase I activities be needed?

- Should the organization form an NAC (explain what this is), and if so, what individuals and groups should be involved?

- What resources might the organization be willing to commit to the needs assessment (think of Phase I at this time, but bring up some Phase II and III activities)?

- How much time would a full Phase I implementation require?

- What is the importance to the organization of looking at needs and ultimately changing what it does in accord with what might be learned?

Give the summary to a few individuals with whom you have been dealing to see if it is on target. Is it clear, especially in regard to what might be done next?

1b. Come to Agreement on What Should Be Done Next

Go back to the total original group that is pushing for the needs assessment with the revised summary and talk about subsequent steps and activities. Generally this will consist of decisions such as the following:

- No more actions are required, and there is not a compelling argument to explore this area or set of concerns further.

- The organization would benefit by entering into Phase I and providing funds for subsequent phases should they be warranted.

- More extensive Phase I work may lead to Phase II activities, and the organization must be aware that this could be an outcome.

- We have learned enough to move to Phase III directly without having to collect additional data/information.

Construct a Memorandum of Agreement

Shouldn't this be done earlier? Its placement here might seem odd, but prior to this there might not be enough information to construct the memorandum. Some reconnaissance is in order before knowing exactly what might be required and what are the critical tasks before a memorandum of agreement can be formulated. If you are external, incorporate some up-front costs into the memorandum. Assuming that a decision is made to proceed with Phase I activities, address the following items:

- the formation of an NAC, its size and composition (what groups should be represented and why), and a strategy for contacting/involving members;

- a schedule of potential meetings of the NAC and what it might be doing (due to scheduling it may be better to have a relatively small committee);

- what kinds of existing data the committee will locate and digest;

- what assistance might be available from the organization and what assistance might come from other groups and organizations (librarians, regional planning commissions, etc.);

- what costs might be associated with assistance and whether current budgets will cover them or some can be donated (get firm commitments);

- what report(s) will be produced from the work of the NAC, as well as approximate dates for them (suggest length, keeping in mind that they should be short);

- to whom reports and oral summaries will be provided;

- what the overall timetable for Phase I might be; and

- an estimate of the funds necessary for the phase.

The title "Memorandum of Agreement" rather than "Contract" is intentional. It is a flexible document, not a binding contract. What happens in needs assessment is that the work can move in unanticipated directions. For example, the data collected in Phase I may yield sufficient information to render Phase II activities unnecessary, or focus might shift to the planning of solution strategies. A memorandum is better for dealing with ambiguities and uncertainties.

Step 2: Forming the NAC and Initial NAC Activities (See Figure 3.2)

2a. Selecting NAC Members

Reconnaissance is paying dividends. Ask the individuals you have been meeting with to offer suggestions for NAC members. Have them respond independently and see if there is a pattern to those being named. Are the same persons being mentioned (a cross-nomination process)? Guide them in the nomination process:

- Are potential nominees knowledgeable about the area of emphasis and where information regarding it might be located?

- Do they represent a reasonable balance of stakeholders or groups with interests in the topic and what might eventually result from the needs assessment?

- Are they a mix of people who are internal and external to the organization?

- Are they individuals who not only have opinions and insights about the topic but who will be active doers of committee work (the NAC is an advisory body and a working committee that participates in data collection, analysis, and interpretation)?

- Do the nominees have a reputation for an openness about their views but not being dogmatic and obstructing progress?

- Do they have special skills (data analysis and manipulation, expertise and experience in the area of focus) that will benefit the effort?

Figure 3.2   Step 2: Forming the NAC and Initial NAC Activities

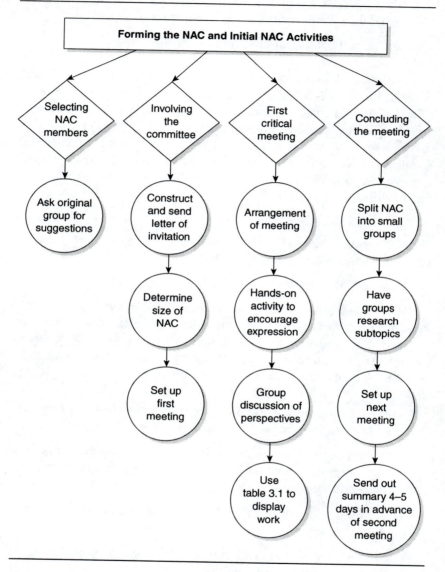

For additional characteristics of NAC members, see Altschuld and Lepicki (2009b, in press).

2b. Contacting and Involving the Committee

Send the potential members a letter of invitation from a recognized organizational leader. It should include:

- the purpose of the needs assessment in helping the organization progress and improve;

- the importance of the work and why their participation is needed;

- how they were identified;

- what is expected from them and what they might be doing;

- an approximate number of meetings (usually 4–5) and the time period in which they will be held (see Ricard & Brendel, 2004, for rough estimates of the time required for an assessment);

- when they will be contacted to ascertain their willingness to serve and possible dates when a first meeting might be held; and

- an expression of appreciation for their consideration of the request.

As noted elsewhere, it is either a large NAC that is split into manageable subgroups to carry out assignments or a smaller one that is easier to convene and orchestrate. If the effort involves a topic of major importance and resolving needs requires sizeable expenditures, then probably a large NAC is better. If the needs are of lesser import, then a smaller one is OK.

With more members, scheduling problems increase exponentially, and since regular attendance at Phase I meetings is critical, a smaller NAC would suffice. NACs succeed if members are dedicated and attend. Contact possible members to solicit involvement and determine meeting times.

2c. That First Critical Meeting

The details of this meeting are important. Refreshments, location, travel reimbursements, and so forth are little things that make for a positive experience and demonstrate to the NAC the seriousness with which the needs assessment is viewed. Key agenda items are as follows:

- Introduce yourself as the facilitator and the charge to the group.

- Ask that members provide *short* introductions to themselves (some of them may already know each other) and make sure that they print their names in large letters on both sides of paper name tents.

- Ask if group members have previously been part of a needs assessment, a strategic planning effort, or another form of identifying and exploring problems (and what such activities looked like).

- Provide additional background on why they were chosen, specific purposes, the area of focus, and other related items.

- Approximate the number of meetings and when they will occur (scheduling has been mitigated through the earlier contacts).

- If you feel that they may not fully understand what is meant by need or needs assessment, provide a few fact sheets that contain basic definitions and examples of needs and/or types of needs as in Chapter 1 (emphasize that needs are gaps or problems, but for now the NAC will not be dealing with solutions).

Now it is time for an activity to get the NAC in tune with basic concepts. Book 2 of the KIT contains several such activities. Review and use them as they fit the local situation. Other examples are:

- short questionnaires that you can construct to get members of the NAC to write down their ideas about the focus of the needs assessment;

- group involvement in a fun and useful exercise based on "The Case of the Pokey Elevators" (Exhibit 3.1); and

- if future needs are of concern, finding or developing brief scenarios about events affecting the future and having the NAC offer suggestions as to what this might mean for the organization.

A short questionnaire is easily and quickly produced. It encourages the NAC to express its thoughts and perceptions about the topic of concern and should include a few mostly open-ended questions that become the basis for exchanging views. It gets the group going and might begin with a brief description (a paragraph or so) of the topic followed by thought-provoking probes:

- What do you think about the current status or performance?

- What should performance be?

- What are some problems or issues that confront us here?

- Which groups and individuals are now receiving services, and are there others that should be?

- Are there services that should be provided but are not?

- What factors seem to facilitate what we currently are doing?

- What factors inhibit efforts in this area?

NAC members jot down their thoughts, and a discussion is begun to gauge commonalities and differences. Summarize their perceptions.

"The Case of the Pokey Elevators" is a humorous approach to starting the process and helps a group to understand a subtle issue in needs assessment, the tendency to jump to solution strategies before fully understanding the problem and what might be causing it. To use "The Case" first have individuals cover up the part of it immediately after the initial diagram with a sheet of paper. Then have them jot down their thoughts about the elevators: What's going on here, what is the problem, and what comes to mind?

Invariably, responses go like this—put in more elevators, have some elevators only go to the top floors and some to the lower floors, encourage people to walk up or down without using the elevator, start a walking-for-health campaign, and so on. Then they read the rest of "The Case," and slowly chuckles are observed around the room. Use their responses to reinforce the concept of need and needs assessment before going to solution strategies.

Exhibit 3.1   The Case of the Pokey Elevators

Once upon a time, a very responsible manager of a twenty-story office building in New York City was besieged by complaints from his tenants. "The elevators are too slow," they complained in a chorus. Being a responsible manager, he immediately called an engineering firm to have a look at the problem. During a preliminary discussion, this rough floor plan was drawn.

Figure 1

Office	Corridor	Elev.	Office
Office			Office
Office			Office
Office			Office

(Continued)

(Continued)

After an exhaustive study utilizing stopwatches and traffic flow charts, the engineering firm gave him a proposal for the installation of two newer and faster elevators in the existing shafts. The price tag was $100,000 for an average time gain of 3.35 minutes from top to bottom for each elevator. This shaved an average of twenty seconds off the waiting time on each floor. "My, that's a lot of money," he said, "and twenty seconds is not a lot of time. I'll let you know."

Since he was also responsible to the building owners, he called another firm. After another exhaustive study, they made their proposal. What he should do, they said, was leave the present elevators alone and add two new elevators at the ends of the central corridor like this:

Figure 2

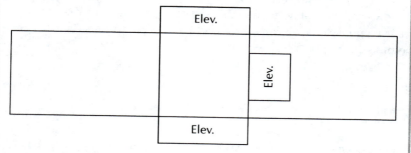

This solution, they said, would cost a little more, $150,000 to be precise, but would save tenants much more time, i.e., an average of 35 seconds shaved off the waiting time on each floor. "My, that would do the trick," he said uneasily, "but, I will have to consult the owners. I'll let you know."

Now, this is the sad part. He knew the owners would not spend that much, and the complaints were growing louder and more angry. In a fever he went to the Yellow Pages looking for someone to help him with his problem. His eyes skimmed down the page:

—"Probabilities"

—"Probers"

—"Problem Consultants"

"That's what I need," he said, "a problem consultant!" He quickly dialed the number.

Now this problem consultant was a strange dude. He practically went to sleep while the building manager described the problem and for the next couple of days, he wandered aimlessly through the building doing nothing as far as the building manager could see. On the third day, he wandered into the manager's office and slouched into a chair.

"Well," he began, "you told me that your problem was slow elevators. What that said to me was that your solution to tenant complaints was faster elevators. But that wasn't really your problem. What those folks were trying to tell you is that they are bored stiff while waiting for the elevators. That's your real problem."

So for less than $1,000, mirrors were installed beside the elevators on every floor. Women straightened their hair, men their ties. There were no more complaints.

Source: From *Planning, Conducting, and Evaluating Workshops,* by L. N. Davis and E. McCallon, 1974, Austin, TX: Learning Concepts.

Now, the committee is primed for needs assessment work. Through materials previously collected, what was learned from initial reconnaissance, or what was learned from the group discussion, begin to identify subtopics or concerns within the main topic, what might be standards or expectations ("what should be"), what the group knows or doesn't know about the current status or situation, sources of information about the two conditions, and where that information or those data might be located. If standards are available (test norms, comparative achievement, market share numbers, quality of goods produced, clients successfully and unsuccessfully treated, national goals for training and specified learning that should result, task/job analyses), provide them to the group.

Keep the discussion on track and frequently summarize on flip charts, overheads, or a quickly generated PowerPoint presentation. What issues or concerns are most important and potentially the subject for further exploration? With 12 members, the NAC could be divided into thirds with one group having Level 1 as its emphasis and the second and third groups dealing with Levels 2 and 3, respectively. Or they all could focus on one of the levels depending on where the process seems to be going. As the discussion proceeds, probe to see what the issues are and if there is general agreement on them. If the group drifts into solutions, don't discourage this but simply maintain a list (a parking lot of these) for later review and redirect its attention to needs.

It's amazing what structured groups like this can produce. But that is to be anticipated because homework is done in the beginning of Phase I by learning as much as you can about the topic, and the NAC consists of individuals who should be able to contribute because of their familiarity with the area of concern and the organization. This works in favor of a positive outcome. If the group members are not chosen well, a rich outcome may not be realized.

What is missing is a way for capturing what is being generated by the NAC. Most procedures follow a generic pattern as in Table 3.1. A table like this (modify as needed) could be used with the large group to summarize what is being derived and be given to each small group to fill in as it proceeds with its deliberations.

The value of the table is underscored. It pulls together what has transpired in the meeting as a guide to further needs assessment activity. It gives a picture of what has been discussed and tells the NAC where the information exists within the system or where it might be located external to the organization. It gets the NAC to thinking about what concerns are there and what will have to be collected to learn more about them.

Another feature of the table is that most of the data tend to be in available sources rather than from new ones. These are the archival class of methods given in Chapter 2. Other data collection procedures for Phase I might be used, but for the most part that work will be minimal. Separate tables for Levels 1, 2, and 3 could be generated and discussed by the large group for deletions, additions, and so on. Such tables can have many versions. Needs assessment procedures are flexible and designed with the local context in mind.

One slight disadvantage that the facilitator should be aware of is that so many areas and subareas might arise that the large group or the small ones lose concentration, dissipate energy, or come to feel that the needs and the entire enterprise are overwhelming. So even at this early stage in the process, some informal prioritization takes place, and the NAC will naturally work with the higher-priority areas and subareas within them.

Table 3.1   One Useful Format for Displaying the Initial Work of the NAC

Area of Concern	What Should Be	What Is	Sources of Information	What We'd Like to Know	Sources of Information
Area 1 Subarea Subarea	Standards, expectations	Current status	Records, archives	More about status, perceptions of status, etc.	Other records, interviews, etc.
Area 2 Subarea Subarea Subarea					
Area *n*					

2d. Concluding the Meeting and Next Steps

Ending with just the table would be a successful but insufficient result. A great deal of brainstorming has occurred and is showing up on the table(s) in rough form. How good was this work? Will existing data provide meaningful insights about areas in the table? Do the data actually exist? In what form are they, and what is their quality? Do the data illuminate whether a need is really there and what its nature might be? What about the entries where the group did not know much and desires to learn more?

Now the NAC is split into three or four small groups with assignments of finding the source of data, what form they are in, and how accessible they are. As the NAC locates information, it is provided between the first and second meetings to the facilitator for insertion into the initial table(s). The data come from databases, existing lists of organizational resources, previous reports, the literature, a sampling of records, and a few interviews.

Set a time for the next meeting—2–4 weeks after the first one. The interim period should be sufficient for knowledgeable NAC members to find materials and data but not so long that they lose momentum. Send electronic summaries of what is happening about 4–5 days in advance of the second meeting.

Step 3: The Next Several Meetings of the NAC (See Figure 3.3)

3a. Continuing to Complete Table(s)

The NAC has gone from being an advisory committee to being active in collecting information related to needs. As the table(s) are being completed, empty or partially filled cells represent a lack of knowledge or the desire to learn more.

The facilitator fills in the table(s) from information found by the NAC. The expanded version(s) are critical input for the second meeting. In preparation for it, the facilitator might do the following:

- maintain both the original and newer table(s) to help the NAC gauge progress being made and what else has to be done;

- develop an agenda for the meeting; and

- generate a list of questions to guide discussion around what is known and in what areas additional data should be sought.

Distribute the questions and agenda to the NAC prior to the meeting so it can consider where the process is and what to do next.

Figure 3.3 Step 3: The Next Several Meetings of the NAC

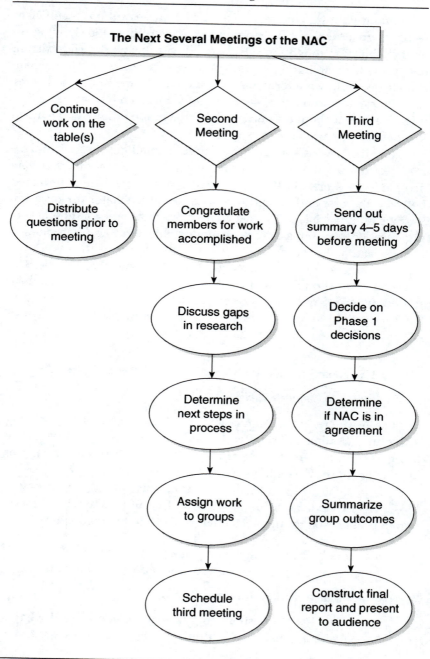

3b. Conduct the Second Meeting

This is where needs assessment gets exciting! Progress is visually evident. The NAC has accomplished much in a relatively short time. Go over what has been learned and where gaps in knowledge still exist. Raise more questions:

- Do we feel comfortable enough in certain areas with what is there, and would more data collection be useful or a waste of time?

- Where should we continue the data collection efforts (are there major areas to do so, and where might key sources be)?

- Are there some areas that require new data (Phase II) since there are no existing or insufficient sources in quality and substance?

- Are there other ideas (causal factors, possible solutions, barriers to solutions) picked up in the process of collecting data?

Although the focus in Phase I is not on causality or solutions, they have arisen and will be useful for later work. This is where that "parking lot" comes to the fore. During the meeting ask NAC members about such features and record their thoughts for subsequent referral.

Lastly, as the NAC examines where it is in the process, lead it toward next steps. It is possible yet unlikely that enough will have been obtained to complete Phase I, to make decisions about Phase II or Phase III actions, or to terminate the endeavor as not being worth further time, money, and energy. It usually takes another meeting with associated data collection in the intervening period before decisions are made. Attain consensus in the NAC for next steps, assign the work, and schedule the third meeting 2–3 weeks from this date.

All interim periods in the text are approximations with variations expected due to the scope and complexity of the needs assessment. Much more time would be required for one of national scope or for one that had complicated data sets needing specialized expertise beyond that of the NAC. Individuals with requisite skills would have to be involved with funds allocated for such purposes. Timelines are adjusted, and as cited before, there has to be budget flexibility in needs assessment. (Note: Phase I is predicated on three NAC meetings after initial reconnaissance and selection of the NAC; depending on the specific situation, more may be necessary. The number is determined by how quickly the assessment can be focused and the availability and accessibility of data and ease of analysis and synthesis.)

3c. *Conduct the Third Meeting of the NAC*

Follow the same procedure used between the first and second meetings and produce a summary of how the NAC was formed, the general process for Phase I activities, what transpired in the initial and follow-up meetings (attach agendas), key areas identified for further Phase I attention, collection of data, and the building of the table(s). Send this out as it is produced, along with new information about 4–5 days before the next meeting. Date the tables.

Now the whole process is in high gear.

- What gaps are apparent in our table?

- Are the needs of sufficient strength to propose doing anything more?

- Should we go to Phase II and begin generating new data collection mechanisms (surveys, epidemiological studies, interviews, etc.)?

- Is there enough understanding of needs to ask what factors are causing them and which of the factors are not under the aegis of the organization?

- Do we perceive what the needs are for Levels 2 and 3, as related to their provision of services or goods for Level 1?

- Do we sense what might be the highest-priority needs at this time?

- Might it be possible to move directly into Phase III?

The facilitator is moving the NAC to final Phase I decisions. Once the group has examined and discussed the outcomes of its work, see if a consensus is emerging. A straw poll will determine if agreement is there, and in the majority of needs assessments it will be. Where it is not, perhaps the group is disagreeing on a few needs but is in accord for others. Ask if those could be chosen as the focal point for next steps.

It might be useful to resurrect and discuss the parking lot. Seek other ideas about causes of needs and potential solution strategies, keeping in mind that they are preliminary perceptions. Remind the NAC that this is a brainstorming activity, helpful for future input but not the final answer.

The work of the committee will be part of a report made to decision makers who must commit to the next steps recommended by the NAC. It is important to communicate to a larger audience in the organization, in summarized form, what the group has done and outcomes so far. Consider a broader distribution especially if the needs assessment is pertinent to external stake-holding groups.

NAC members should be at the meeting when the final report is presented to decision makers (see Step 4). Other meetings with a wider cross-section of the organization could be scheduled. If some members of the NAC could come to them, it would demonstrate support for findings.

Step 4: The Final Meeting With Decision Makers (See Figure 3.4)

4a. Preparing for the Meeting

The presentation must be carefully organized and build on the thoughtful work of the NAC. Several committee members should

Figure 3.4 Step 4: The Final Meeting With Decision Makers

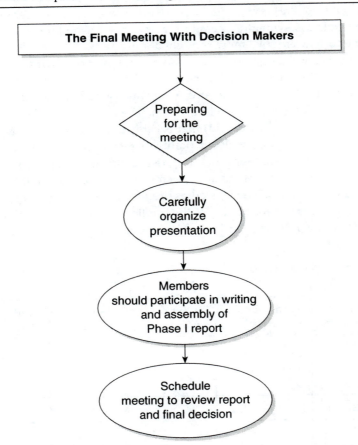

participate in writing and assembling the Phase I report. With agendas, tables, and documentation it is a lasting record of the needs assessment, a history of who was involved, what they did and found, sources of information (a good result by itself), what was recommended and why, and other important things.

Think of all activities related to the investigation of needs as a kind of seamless problem-solving process in the shape of a funnel. It goes from first narrowing the focus to identifying and prioritizing needs, analyzing causes, and concluding with the selection and implementation of a solution to rectify a prioritized subset of needs (problems). It is difficult to avoid blending these steps together in subtle ways no matter how hard we try.

Therefore, why not use everything collected in Phase I, all the formal and more informal information about causes and tentative ideas in relation to solution strategies? Make sure that the tenuous nature is clearly labeled, and issues will have to be explored more subsequently in the needs assessment process, if for no other reason than it is interesting and will provoke more thought about needs.

Table 3.2 was designed with that in mind. Based on the last meeting of the NAC, this table could be fashioned. First, present to those making decisions Table 3.1, which contains what was learned about each of the areas of need and subareas within them. Then provide Table 3.2 with those parts of Table 3.1 (in bold) that became key foci of Table 3.2.

Also provide short bulleted points of recommendations for next actions, why they are being made, possible causes of needs or problems, and potential solution strategies for them. Make sure that the last two entries in Table 3.2 are labeled as preliminary thinking. Engage the decision makers in a discussion of the implications for the organization of what has been learned in Phase I. (Remember to date the tables.)

Table 3.2   A Phase 1 Decision-Oriented Framework

Need Area and Subareas	Further Actions Required	Reasons for Further Action	Preliminary Ideas About Causes and Solutions	
Area 1 Subarea 1 Subarea 2				
Area 2				
Area 3				
Area n				

Suggest that they schedule another meeting to review further what has been done and what they support for continued needs assessment activity. Offer that you and several NAC members could be there to explain facets of what has been done for clarification and explanatory purposes. The decision makers have the final responsibility for decisions about resources, personnel allocations, and future directions.

Highlights of the Chapter

1. NAG, NAG, NAG! Oops—that is, NAC, NAC, NAC! The NAC is the mover of the needs assessment process. Its drive and interest make for success of the effort. This cannot be overemphasized, and the implications of not choosing well and not carefully organizing for how this group functions are obvious.

2. Organization for Phase I is very important. The responsibility for meeting planning, monitoring during interim periods, and presenting the public face of the assessment is that of the facilitator. Stay on top of tasks and maintain contact with the subcommittees as they do their work. The facilitator has three roles in needs assessment—planner, maintainer, and coach.

3. Too often it is assumed that it will take a good deal of time and resources to study needs and to draw action-based conclusions from their results. The assumption is not quite correct. Organizations are frequently awash in information, or external groups can supply much that is relevant. Phase I, by using what exists, thus making the effort easier and preventing needless investment in it.

4. An issue in Phase I is how wide or narrow in scope a needs assessment should be. There are dangers in its being too wide (loss of direction; feelings that nothing will be achieved, that the problems are too great to be resolved, that resource allocations will be spread too thin to make a difference). Narrowing too much may have the effect of not having enough meaning or not leading to changes in the situation and improvement (little good will occur from resolving this small problem; nobody will notice any changes). There are no rules for scope. Trust in the wisdom of the NAC; its members know the heartbeat of the organization, and via their insight, the scope should hopefully be appropriate.

4

Phase II: Assessment

Two Frequently Used Quantitative Approaches

❖ INTRODUCTION

A decision has been made to move into Phase II. More knowledge about needs is required by looking for additional existing data or from new sources of information. Given the costs associated with Phase II, reflect on what has been learned and what might be done next.

At this point remember the roles played by the needs assessment committee (NAC): advisory, helping to focus the assessment and guide the process; participatory, in the collection and analysis of data to the extent feasible (this might include working with specialized experts when they do part of the assessment); and interactive, influencing organizations about next steps with regard to needs. All roles are of value with the NAC an integral part of all of them from start to finish. Phase II now begins.

❖ STEP 1: ORIENTATION

1a. Reconvene the NAC

Contact the NAC membership, explain the decision to move to Phase II, and see if they are willing to continue. Ideally, everyone will be. Chemistry has developed, and they have a feel for when to challenge each other, go for consensus, and get down to work. Hopefully all will stay, but be prepared to replace a few with similar individuals (look at others nominated in Phase I but not chosen). Employ the same procedures used previously to get new members.

1b. Planning for the First NAC Meeting of Phase II

See what dates are feasible for the first meeting and schedule accordingly. There are many activities in Phase II, but much was learned from Phase I that has an impact on what the NAC will do here. Indeed some steps could be omitted or given little attention with no adverse effect on the needs assessment and a positive one on the budget.

Send a summary of what was done before. Focus the agenda on key questions:

- Was enough found out about the areas of interest (the discrepancies) that expensive new data are not warranted?
- Do we have a solid sense of the discrepancies for each of the three levels (service recipients, providers, and the organizational system)?
- Are we clear and in agreement as to which needs are the priorities of the committee and the organization?
- Should the focus shift to what is causing needs and determining final needs-based priorities, taking into account what the organization can and cannot do?
- Should we develop criteria for choosing and/or developing or locating solution strategies?
- Do we know enough to jump directly into Phase III?

These are the normal questions covered in Phase II. There are others, less frequently asked, which could also be of major concern:

- What are the internal and external risks for the organization in resolving needs or not attending to them?
- What resources could be assigned to meet the need or be obtained (where are they, and how might they be accessed)?

1c. The First Meeting

Welcome everyone, describe prior work, and lead a discussion of at least the first set of questions raised above. From there, the group could be divided into thirds to take a look at the questions for Levels 1, 2, and 3, respectively.

Small-group members could use Table 4.1, individually and then together, to generate a summary to be shared, altered, and agreed upon by the larger group. When the total group is looking at the tables, the small groups offer explanations about whether the tables will make sense when scrutinized by decision makers and others in the organization and whether they provide a strong basis for further action and commitment of resources. The facilitator establishes the atmosphere for all discussions and provides ground rules for them. The tone of exchanges in discussions should be expansive, not defensive.

The NAC is not a decision-making body, but what it produces affects decisions. The organization (leadership, personnel, and stakeholders) has the ultimate say as to what it will do with recommended actions. Table 4.1 helps the NAC sort out perceptions and what underlies them. The NAC may rank its ideas to highlight the most prominent ones and avoid their getting lost in the mix with those of lesser prominence.

Take a moment to think about Table 4.1 and others prepared earlier. Again, if placed in *dated order*, a progression would be evident from the initial steps of the needs assessment to what is currently a more

Table 4.1 Focusing Phase II (Assessment) Activities

Potential Next Steps in Phase II					
Area of Concern	*What We Know*	*More Knowledge Desirable*	*Causal Analysis*	*Possible Solution Criteria*	*Possible Solutions*
Area 1 Subarea 1 Subarea 2	Level 1 Level 2 Level 3 Level 1 Level 2 Level 3				
Area 2					
Area 3					
Area *n*					

selective focus. Use of the dated tables to communicate to stakeholders is strongly encouraged. Besides having communicative value, they are the permanent record of the process. They are essential elements of the chronological documentation of the entire effort.

At this point, to a partial degree and informally, the NAC has been gently establishing priorities for its work as well as for the organization. In many assessments, priority-setting procedures may not be required, whereas in others they are required, as will be explained later in this book.

The NAC via Table 4.1 has a good sense for what lies ahead. It will be doing all or any one of the following four activities: collecting more information about areas of need and discrepancies, prioritizing needs, causally analyzing them, and defining and/or identifying possible solution strategies. Each of these actions will be looked at in terms of what it entails. There are many ways to collect information about needs other than using archived sources. Experienced needs assessors employ multiple methods, qualitative and quantitative (Ricard & Brendel, 2004). With multiple methods, costs will rise, and it will be more difficult to implement the assessment and derive common meaning across results. On the other hand, this strategy is used because the complexity of some needs mandates an examination from varied perspectives.

The most frequently observed qualitative methods are the focus group interview, nominal group technique, community (group) forum, and personal interview. Quantitatively, aside from archived sources, surveys predominate, and in some fields, epidemiological studies are notable. Few facilitators have in-depth knowledge of all of the approaches in Chapter 2 (Table 2.3) and the subtle features that make for success in applying them. Therefore, if specialized strategies are necessary, there should be sufficient resources for experts with the skills and experience for implementing them.

A general outline will be given for two frequently utilized quantitative approaches for collecting new information about needs. More details are in other books in the KIT or additional sources. Table 4.2 provides brief overviews of the commonly encountered quantitative methods.

❖   STEP 2: COLLECTING NEW INFORMATION
     ABOUT NEEDS VIA SURVEYS

2.1 NAC Meetings During Most of Data Collection

In Phase II, the NAC does much of its work through subcommittees that schedule their own meetings. The facilitator may have to prod and/or encourage the groups to stay on task. Full committee meetings

Table 4.2 Phase II Quantitative Needs Assessment Methods

Methods		
Aspect	*Survey*	*Epidemiology*	*Other Methods*
Purpose	Determine the perspective of groups about need areas Obtain ratings of as well as open-ended comments about needs	Compare the current prevalence of a disease (or situation) with the future incidence of that disease (or situation)	There are numerous other quantitative techniques that are applied in Phase II and in Phase I such as task analyses, risk assessments, etc., to ascertain needs Some specialized methods are used for more future-oriented needs assessments
Ease of implementation	Relatively easy with some know-how	Relatively difficult without specialized training and analytical skills	Depends on the method with some being relatively easy and others complex and difficult
Cost considerations	Moderate to low if the survey works well, medium to high if it doesn't	Moderate but will be higher if special data collection is required such as surveys and/or interviews	Generally inexpensive unless intensive fieldwork becomes necessary such as in certain task analyses
Value of information obtained	Moderate to high	Moderate to high and in some areas (disease, human resource projections, etc.) very high	Moderate to high depending on the circumstances and what the data requirements of the situation are
Issues	The majority of needs assessment surveys do not use the necessary double scaling Return rates can be low, and results may be skewed or biased	Usually complex in terms of statistics Estimates can be off especially as applied to fields other than health	For some of these methods, good examples are not found in the literature such as the coupling of needs and risk assessments Overall used less frequently than surveys

occur in the process, as necessary. Only the one that occurs near the end of the phase is discussed in the next chapter.

2.2 Conducting Surveys

Surveys are the most used/abused method for obtaining information about needs. Witkin (1994) noted that most needs assessment surveys consisted of only one dimension, thus violating the principle that need is a measurable discrepancy between what is and what should be. Why this is the case is not clear, and we will provide a way to partially overcome this deficiency.

The steps for conducting surveys go something like this:

2.2.1 Determine if the survey is a good way to proceed by thinking about the following:

- Is information about needs required from a cross-section of concerned or involved individuals, and will it be unique or different from what we already know?

- Is there enough interest in the topic so that surveys will be returned in sufficient numbers and reasonably well completed?

- Are there adequate resources and time for the development, implementation, analysis, and interpretation of the survey?

- Will the surveys be worth the effort (the bottom line)?

If the answers are yes, it is expected that there is familiarity with survey methods—therefore the purpose is to highlight features of them pertinent to the needs assessment context (Figure 4.1).

2.2.2 Who should be surveyed, and how should they be surveyed?

Include individuals from groups with vested interests in the outcomes and who are able to offer useful insights about needs. Individuals from Levels 1, 2, and 3 could be included with separate versions of the survey developed for the unique aspects of each (terms each level uses when referring to needs, its relationship to the area, audience sophistication). A representative sample of the groups should be selected and contacted in a way to ensure adequate return (cover letter appeal, questionnaire design, etc.).

Mail the survey to a random sample of individuals from designated groups or use Web-based approaches (many are commercially

Figure 4.1 Steps for Conducting Surveys

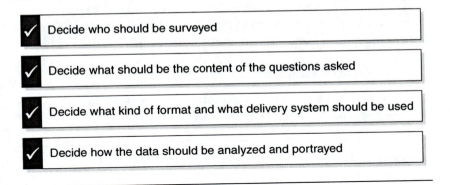

✓ Decide who should be surveyed

✓ Decide what should be the content of the questions asked

✓ Decide what kind of format and what delivery system should be used

✓ Decide how the data should be analyzed and portrayed

available) to deliver the survey. No matter how access is done, the importance of the respondent's role in supplying data is always underscored in communications. Lastly, it is worthwhile to send out a brief summary of results to respondents when it becomes available. This is potentially helpful for public relations.

Sometimes it may be desirable to use the survey with intact groups: classrooms, community group meetings, the workforce in one location, conferences, or other places where individuals are naturally congregated. Example 4.1 contains a clever use of a specialized forum for survey delivery.

Example 4.1

Making Methods Do Double Duty

A school district took advantage of a series of community group meetings to collect survey data. Toward the end of each meeting, which usually involved spirited and open discussions from groups of about 50, a survey was administered. Attendees responded to alternative strategies for resolving the district's pressing educational problem—serious growth and the associated overcrowding that was occurring in its single, very large high school. On the survey, each option with its costs was included. In this manner, the district obtained nearly 1,000 responses from community members (out of a total population of 35,000). The district reduced expenses by obtaining data from the discussions and the survey at the same time. One issue was that those in attendance may have been representative not of the district but of more self-selected groups.

2.2.3 What should be the content of the questions?

Do not ask broad, overarching questions; focus on specific concerns such as opinions emanating from personal experience with, involvement in, and/or interest in an entity. For example:

- How often does and should this behavior occur?

- To what extent should communication take place in our organization, and to what extent does it?

- What are your present levels of skills regarding aspects of the job, and what should they be?

- What features might lead to success of a process or procedure, and are they present in the organization?

2.2.4 What kind of format and survey administration should be used?

As noted, most needs assessment surveys do not usually ask about the "what should be" and "what is" states, the two conditions necessary for a need. Based on the definition, double-scaled instruments (more rarely, triple and quadruple scaling with categories like feasibility and/or cost considerations in resolving needs, motivation to change) are now more often used. In Figure 4.2 is an illustration of a double scale (Hamann, 1997). The item stem is on the left, and the scales are on the right. The stem could also be in the middle with the "what should be" side on the right and the "what is" on the left, and with three or more scales, array them to the right of the stem.

Wording of the scales in most assessments deals with importance (the "what should be") and achievement (the "what is"). A better way to construct such scales almost has the same phrasing for both conditions as in the figure.

Why are these features being stressed? The clustering on the same side of the page with *more than two* scales is visually appealing. Putting the stem in the middle with several scales to the left and right seems to fracture the view and may lead to lower completion rates. (Since Hamann, 1997, found that rates were lower for double-scaled items, even for sophisticated audiences, make the survey pleasing to the eye.)

The concern over the phrasing is important. Discrepancy scores are fraught with problems, one being the subtraction of one score from another. Both scores have error in them, thus compounding it in the discrepancy score. A second issue is whether the subtraction makes logical and intuitive sense. Subtracting achievement from importance

Figure 4.2 A Format for Double-Scaled Needs Assessment Items

Mental Health	To what extent									
Well-Being Areas	Should we be measuring these areas?					Are we measuring these areas?				
Area 1	1	2	3	4	5	1	2	3	4	5
Area 2	Repeat the scaling options for each mental health area									
Area 3										
Area *n*										

creates a discrepancy from inherently different types of responses. This problem is seldom discussed in the literature of needs assessment.

We offer a partial solution. Keeping the wording similar makes the idea of subtraction more palatable. The "what should be" and "what is" in Figure 4.2 are close in wording. This is not a perfect solution, but we think it works better. Consider it for your survey!

Incorporate (limit the number to two to four) open-ended questions in the survey so that the burden of analysis will not be too great. With many such questions and a large sample, the analysis work rises dramatically, even with qualitative analysis computer packages.

2.2.5 How should the data be analyzed and portrayed?

Here are some easy procedures with high utility for needs assessment and for decision making. One is Means Difference Analysis (MDA). Calculate the means for all items that make up the "what should be" and "what is" sides of the equation. Then subtract the latter from the former, generating a standard discrepancy to which the difference for each individual item is compared.

Suppose the "what should be" average is 4.15 and the "what is" average is 2.95 (4.15 − 2.95 = 1.2); the difference of 1.2 units is a standard. Items exceeding this value are needs (indicated with a + in a column of a table where "what should be" and "what is" values are shown for each item). Although needs assessment scales are mostly Likert in nature, the usage of means predominates. One could substitute median values to create the standard.

There are other considerations to think about when using MDA. If the instrument contains subsections, it might be best to do an MDA for each one. Second, if many + signs appear, the NAC could increase the size of the standard or designate some sections as being of more importance. Third, when two items have the same MDA value, a higher "what should be" score is the basis for selecting one over another. Fourth, if the current level of achievement is greater than the desired status, it may signal that resources should be reduced for an area or that inquiry into what is causing the result is warranted. Finally, the idea of computing a mean across individual items that are unique as opposed to a cohesive scale may not be a reasonable strategy to employ.

Summarize open-ended data by looking for themes in the responses (see Book 3 for more details). When quantitative and qualitative data are corroborative or when one expands understanding of the other, that fact should be emphasized in reports. With qualitative data, include some quotes to bring a theme to life and to ensure that the intensity of the original comments is not lost in sanitized themes (see Example 4.2).

Example 4.2

Let the Kids Do the Talking!

A mostly scaled questionnaire was sent to participants in a program that assisted students from an urban district in pursuing postsecondary educational opportunities. Several open-ended questions were included, one of which probed the value of postsecondary education to the individual, almost a retrospective needs assessment. The data readily fell into themes (monetary benefits, opportunities to grow, exploring new horizons, exposure to other people and cultures). For the verbal presentation to the program's prominent advisory board, a summary of themes was prepared but not used.

What, the themes weren't used? The themes could not capture the emotion and the earthy vernacular of the students. The first two pages of the open-ended responses (expletives included) were distributed to board members for silent reading. The room became still, and when finished the board members were asked if it would be useful to look at the summarized themes. From their body language, the unanimous answer was no. The statements, in the words of the "Kids," made the point much better than the evaluators ever could.

One approach to display results, aside from very direct and easily constructed MDA tables, is provided in Table 4.3. This is a slightly more sophisticated version of the tables sometimes used with needs data. The cells in the upper right-hand corner are the ones that truly indicate need—the "what should be" scores are high, and the "what is"

Table 4.3 Showing Double-Scaled Needs Data

"What Should Be" Scale (1 = low value and 5 = high value)						
		1	2	3	4	5
The "What Is" Scale (1–5)	1					Cell 1, 5— absolute need
	2					
	3					
	4					
	5	Cell 5, 1— no need				

scores are low. In a sense, the other cells for double-scaled surveys don't matter much. A high "what should be" coupled with a high "what is" score does not indicate need, and a high "what is" with a low "what should be" is a candidate for reductions in resources or detailed scrutiny. Only items whose responses fall into the upper right-hand corner of the table require attention.

Calculate an MDA value and build a simple table showing the item averages for the two dimensions of needs, the discrepancy between them, and whether or not the discrepancy was greater than the MDA. After that is done, place the item numbers of those whose response pattern tends to fall into the upper right corner of Table 4.3. The NAC would first look at the items that fell closest to Cell 1, 5 (Row 1 and Column 5). Compare the MDA table with Table 4.3, and it should be easy to see the high-priority needs.

❖ STEP 3: COLLECTING NEW INFORMATION ABOUT NEEDS VIA EPIDEMIOLOGY

Epidemiology is a specialized way of dealing with data coming from health-related fields. It requires trained professionals and may substantially increase the costs and time for a needs assessment. It can be complicated and with admittedly more of a surface type of treatment given in this text. The reason for including it and briefly mentioning some other strategies is that they are not as frequently seen in education, social work, and so forth, but they should be.

Epidemiology deals with the prevalence of a disease, how many people have it now, and an estimate of its incidence—how many will get it in the future, essentially the "what will be" state. Once discrepancies are determined over time, epidemiologists look at what might be producing or leading to the negative futures or undesirable outcomes. It is a form of and has powerful uses for needs assessment. Good illustrations of this technique appear frequently in the everyday press. Strobbe (2009) has written about the rise of chlamydia infections, and Fuhrmans (2009) has reported on the shortage of general surgeons. Both articles have many features of the epidemiological approach. Going further, Price (2008) cautioned that archived data useful for epidemiology have to be carefully examined in regard to how they are coded or entered into a database. She noted that this is particularly true for accurately capturing murder-suicide cases.

Consider epidemics such as AIDS, the potential of avian flu, or the rise in diabetes of all forms and most troubling the increasing levels of juvenile diabetes or juveniles with the onset of adult diabetes. AIDS was a rapidly growing major health scare (and still is) that Western societies began seeing 20 years ago and that is pandemic now in some areas of the world. It is appearing in ominous dimensions in Africa, Asia, and Eastern Europe.

Epidemiologists studied the disease, learned about its transmission, and became concerned about how fast it could spread and, if unchecked, ravage a population. They noted its growth and sought to find out what was causing the disease and its propagation. In the latter regard they found a link that if attended to could ameliorate the rate of increase. If those with the disease were to continue having unprotected intercourse, the effects of increasing incidence could be projected with devastating impact on individuals, countries, and even cultures.

Epidemiology requires the collection of an extensive set of data about a disease over a lengthy period of time. Epidemiologists must have in-depth knowledge of how a disease functions, how it is transmitted/contracted, ways to project its spread (rates of persons infected), and health behaviors. The databases are characterized by careful planning, especially in terms of key variables measured and how data regarding them are obtained and entered into the system. (Beyond the databases, epidemiology also requires other kinds of investigative work to understand disease.)

With multiple important (and selectively chosen) variables in the base and with the capabilities of modern multivariate statistics, it is possible to identify (tease out) probable causal pathways leading to disease. Since there are thousands of cases at hand, hypotheses and pathways can be tested via one random sample and confirmed independently through another. Because data are collected on a regular basis, trends can be noted and monitored.

Using this approach, Chiasera (2005) and Chiasera, Taylor, Wolf, and Altschuld (2008) identified a 1%–2% increase in a 5-year period in the number of children in the United States ages 5–19 who were either overweight or at risk for being overweight (other references emanating from this research are Chiasera, Taylor, Wolf, and Altschuld, 2007a, 2007b, and Taylor, Wolf, and Chiasera, 2006). Chiasera provided analyses potentially predictive of a linkage to the later occurrence of diabetes.

In many cases, such data are collected nationally as in the National Health and Nutrition Examination Survey (NHANES, 2004) and cancer registries or in education in the National Education Longitudinal Study (NELS). NHANES is an expensive but very worthwhile endeavor. Data come from representative samples by means of surveys and specially designed and elaborate mobile testing centers that obtain data on weight, lifestyles, food consumed by individuals, family histories, blood factors, and a host of related variables. It is a mechanism for assessing the pulse beat and the health of America's youth. (See Book 3 for more about Chiasera's work and the database.)

From the perspective of epidemiology, what might be applications in education and other fields? Consider the following example (see Example 4.3).

Example 4.3

Epidemiology in Education

Think about teacher shortages in science and mathematics. We could examine the ages of teachers, retirement rates, how soon teachers at older ages were thinking abut retiring (via surveys and interviews), new teachers coming into the field, the numbers being trained in universities who then enter the teaching profession, the number who stay in it for a sizable period of time, the numbers who leave prematurely from more difficult teaching environments, science and mathematics education standards and requirements and how changes in them may affect the need for teachers, birth rates and the demographics of the school-age population, dropout rates, and other factors.

The current status is generated and compared to the projected one to determine replacement needs. As the needs become clear, the analysis prompts thinking about what is causing departures and likely solution

(Continued)

(Continued)

strategies. In this vein, one state projected an emerging teacher shortage in the areas of concern.

In disease, we ask how we can cure the disease or to what extent it can be mitigated or stopped altogether. Analogously, for teacher supply and demand, we could consider how to increase the supply side or how to encourage younger teachers to stay in education and older ones to remain in the classroom until the pipeline of new graduates can be affected. Given that the supply is not quickly ramped up, a way to resolve the problem would be to fill math and science classrooms with less qualified teachers (those who have minored in mathematics or science but are not certified or are minimally certified to teach the content). Unfortunately, teaching out of area occurs more than is desirable and than we would like to admit. It is not an inspired and reasonable solution.

The state in question came up with an imaginative but somewhat costly strategy for resolving the impending dilemma. It provided an incentive for experienced teachers to remain in the classroom. The percentage of pension credit given for staying longer in the classroom was increased substantially. This was an excellent short-term solution to the problem but one with a downside. Costs for the retirement system increased, and the bonus had to be offered to all teachers, not just those in the key areas.

Another use of epidemiology in education is related to fast-growing enrollments. Districts would examine new housing units, numbers and ages of children who might be living in them, potential effects on schools at different levels, the incomes of parents purchasing homes, and so forth. The methodology is based upon existing data as available, in looking for patterns or trends. Then it could be coupled with survey and/or qualitative data collection.

It is not much of a stretch of the imagination to see how the same principles relate to areas as diverse as insurance and autism. Should rates and policies for permanent life insurance be separated for men and women, especially in terms of age (S. Altschuld, personal communications, 2003)? Longevity trends are different for the genders and would affect payout schedules and how policies should be written. Should they take into consideration longevity rates of different subgroups in the United States? Epidemiology would be helpful here via what could be learned from the relevant and enormous sources of extant data. For autism, could we probe into causal factors by the application of epidemiology?

3.1 Initial Thinking Necessary
to Start the Epidemiological Process

Do your circumstances fit this methodological approach, and are resources (fiscal, time, expertise) available to do this kind of a needs assessment study? Consult the literature to see if there are national or local studies for the concerns in your situation. Have any recent ones been done that could be adapted for your case? What variables seemed to be salient? Are local data on them available?

3.2 What Do You Already Know?

Although some aspects of epidemiology may have popped up before in Phase I, let's raise some questions for review:

- What are the sources of supply (in human resources as an example) or what is likely to occur?

- What factors contribute to the above sources?

- Are there data/is there information to project what might take place in the short term?

- Are there data to project what might take place in the longer term regarding programmatic, legislative, and related changes?

- What data are accessible?

- Does our approach to the problem contain pertinent factors and/or variables (see Example 4.3)?

- Do the data collected to date have sufficient specificity for projecting rates of change?

- Is specialized expertise required to conduct the study?

- Do we understand the capacity of the system to meet the positive and negative dimensions of the emerging needs?

3.3 Collect Additional Data as Needed

Aside from the above data, knowledgeable individuals could be interviewed about their perceptions, what they know, what has been found so far, how to interpret existing information, critical dimensions that have been missed, trends likely in the area of interest that might be pertinent, and so on. Other techniques include small-group meetings with those versed in the area, surveying individuals, or conducting a specialized study that ascertains the impact of main factors on each other in the near-term future (the cross-impact method in Witkin & Altschuld, 1995). Many of the previous ideas about surveys could be adapted for use at this time.

3.4 Compile the Data and Estimate Possible Futures as Compared to Present Status

As the data are amassed, note that there are multiple estimates of the incidence for the area of interest. *Don't fixate on one!* Create estimates for what is *most pessimistic*, what is *most likely*, and what is *most optimistic*. Make sure that the assumptions underlying these estimates are transparent. This will be important when they are presented to decision makers.

3.5 Report the Results

Present the results in a summarized and succinct manner. Explain but don't dwell on how estimates were derived. Remember the KISS principle: Make your reports as clear and direct as you can.

Before leaving epidemiology, another interesting case is given in Example 4.4. It is sort of a "what if" that we envision as providing guidance for educators in relation to proficiency testing.

Example 4.4

Epidemiology, Prediction, and Proficiency Testing!

What are the effects of lowering/raising cut points for the proficiency tests that are in virtually every state in the country? With the extensive available databases that have been collected and maintained for many years, would it be possible to project into the short and long term what might happen if the scores were raised or lowered? What impact would there be on pass-fail rates? How many students would drop out, and when would they drop out? What would be the effects on schools, students, and society? What might be public reactions to changing standards—positive and negative impacts on school system performance? What kinds of remedial instruction and/or supplemental services would enable more students to attain the pass score? What costs might be needed to provide such assistance?

Epidemiology fits this kind of circumstance and provides information for policy and practice-oriented decisions. Data analyzed in this way (a combination of epidemiology and trend studies) would be extremely valuable for the deliberations of legislatures and school boards.

❖ STEP 4: COLLECTING NEW INFORMATION
   ABOUT NEEDS VIA OTHER QUANTITATIVE METHODS

Although only two quantitative techniques (surveys and epidemiology with associated trend data) have been described, there have been references made to other quantitative and qualitative methodologies applied in needs assessment studies. (See Table 2.3 and the Other Methods column of Table 4.2.) The reader is referred to publications by Altschuld and Witkin (2000); Gupta (1999); Gupta, Sleezer, and Russ-Eft (2007); McKillip (1987); Witkin and Altschuld (1995); and many others for procedures such as task analyses, specialized futures materials, critical incidence techniques, and so forth.

Highlights of the Chapter

1. Work in Phase II is dependent on Phase I—review of that phase is imperative before expending resources and energy in Phase II.

2. Surveys are one of the most common techniques in needs assessment. It does not take that much effort to make their application more sophisticated and in accord with the discrepancy concept of need. Take the extra time to do so; it is worth it.

3. Epidemiological studies have merit for needs assessment and should be done more often in fields other than health. Strongly consider their value for such assessments.

4. For surveys and epidemiological work, specialized skills may be required. If this is the case, make certain there is flexibility in the original budget or alert decision makers as to what additional resources might be needed.

Next Steps

There are two additional aspects of Phase II—qualitative techniques and making sense of the overall data picture. They are treated in the next chapter.

5

Phase II: The Other Parts of Assessment

Often Used Qualitative Approaches and Pulling the Data Together

❖ FIRST CONSIDERATIONS

As in the prior chapter, the needs assessment committee (NAC) has decided to use quantitative methods, qualitative methods, or both in Phase II. The initial steps explained in Chapter 4 are valid and will not be repeated. Let's examine important qualitative approaches commonly seen in assessments. General guidelines rather than detailed specific steps are given.

A need or a discrepancy from a quantitative perspective is a numeric indication that something is missing; something is wrong and requires attention. But this information is limited and doesn't tell us about how the problem is viewed or understood by those who are concerned with or experiencing it. So it makes sense to combine quantitative and qualitative procedures leading to more in-depth understanding of needs. Doing this is not without issues. First, qualitative approaches do not lead directly to a discrepancy; instead they show what individuals or groups think about problems, concerns, and needs. Second, some needs assessors are attracted to and favor certain methods over others. It is easy to get enamored with surveys or focus group interviews. Avoid such temptations and be open to all types of methodological choices.

❖ STEP 1: SELECTING A QUALITATIVE METHOD

An overview of qualitative techniques for needs assessment is shown in Table 5.1. Three (community groups or community group forums, focus group interviews, and nominal group technique) are described in depth. Choose the method that best fits the local situation.

Table 5.1   Phase II Qualitative Needs Assessment Methods

	Method			
Aspect	Group Forums	Focus Groups	Nominal Groups	Other Methods
Purpose	Determine perceptions of problems, needs, and issues from large groups (>40) Obtain feedback on work done to date	Understand how small, generally homogeneous groups view an issue or area of need Learn how issues and/or needs are referred to as a prelude to survey development	Small-sized groups generate multiple ideas about needs or concerns in a short period of time Obtain priorities about those ideas	Interviews, observations, etc., mostly, but not exclusively, used to collect data on the "what should be" states
Ease of implementation	Seemingly simple, but much behind-the-scenes work Highly dependent on skills and experience of group leader	Straightforward, but care should be taken in selecting the facilitator as to whether the group will open up for that individual	Procedural rules must be followed, or the properties of the technique disappear	While most of the other techniques are easily implemented, they will in some cases require extensive preparation

Aspect	Group Forums	Focus Groups	Nominal Groups	Other Methods
Cost considerations	Relatively inexpensive, but up-front costs for planning, publicity, refreshments, and especially a good external leader	Participants are usually paid a stipend, and appropriate leadership is a must that requires additional expenditure	Relatively inexpensive way to generate ideas	Generally inexpensive, but methods such as mailed Delphi and future scenarios may take extensive amounts of time for return and to develop content
Value of information obtained	High value especially in regard to feedback on directions taken, findings, community views, etc.	High value for understanding frames of reference and/or for the generation of instruments	High value in terms of producing many ideas and the priority of same in a short time period	Can be high depending on what kind of information is required (e.g., the DACUM process and critical incidence technique for task analyses)
Issues	Usually occurs after the fact (i.e., following a number of other activities) and is not a substitute for them Most of the time will not produce discrepancies	Very limited ability to get at discrepancies What people say at a focus group may not relate to how they will act at a later time	Good at generating ideas, but does not yield discrepancy information Discussion only occurs toward the end of the session	Some of the techniques are not often observed in the literature of needs assessment

1.1 General Characteristics of Group Processes

Most of the qualitative methods in needs assessment involve small or large groups. All group procedures require planning, sampling of participants, leading groups, reporting, and the like. In Figure 5.1 these are summarized in outline format.

1.2 Specifics About Group Processes

Unique dimensions for each group process are shown in Figure 5.2.

❖ STEP 2: PUTTING THE DATA TOGETHER

A lot of data and information (qualitative and quantitative) is now available that, if not collated, could be confusing for decision-making purposes. One way to put the data together would be to take advantage of previous summaries that were distributed to the NAC in preparation for deciding on priorities and next steps. Why not just use the tables that have already been completed for this purpose? This is reasonable, but there may be a better idea.

To begin, consider what your multiple sources of data are telling you about needs. Do they agree, partially agree, or disagree? In Table 5.2, such situations are depicted with guidance for how to think about the data.

❖ STEP 3: PORTRAYING THE DATA

Summaries are vital for understanding and arriving at final decisions and priorities. In this vein, a practical approach has been developed by Wilson, Shayne, Lipsey, and Derzon (1996), as illustrated in Table 5.3. The entries in the cells are goal attainment scores. The NAC judges the results from each source (including qualitative ones) on a 5-point scale with 5 being the highest level of need and 1 the lowest. In the table, the four *x*s for the first need stand for the NAC's perception that the survey is a strong indication of need, which is the same for records and even higher for focus group interviews. For Need 2, the data are not as supportive, and for Need 3, the initial high support coming from records was not corroborated by surveys and focus group interviews. Such a table is utilitarian for committee deliberations.

Figure 5.1 Generic Features of Group Procedures in Needs Assessment

---

Planning

Will a group process add knowledge/understanding to warrant its cost?

Will it enhance the credibility of the assessment?

Who should plan and carry it out?

   Who has responsibility for planning since there is much behind-the-scenes work?

   How many groups should be conducted? (Procedures must be replicated to see if findings conform to a pattern and are reliable across sessions. Reliability and validity are enhanced if independent facilitators lead meetings.)

Purposes

What are the specific purposes of the three main procedures?

What do you hope to get out of them?

   A community group forum (CGF) is a moderately large group procedure to obtain feedback on the direction of a needs assessment, a sense of community perceptions about an area, and a sense of issues.

   A focus group interview (FGI) leads to understanding of what a small, homogeneous group of individuals thinks about an issue; what words group members use in referring to it (useful for developing a survey); what individuals might be prone to do regarding a problem; and what they think might be causing it.

   The nominal group technique (NGT) is a small-group technique that rapidly generates and prioritizes ideas and minimizes "groupthink."

How will the results be incorporated into the needs assessment report?

How will data from groups complement other data or show areas of disagreement?

Sampling

What groups should participate in the meetings?

What size should groups be?

   A CGF is a moderately large (40–60 participants) cross-section of concerned citizens or persons influential in organizations with a stake in the areas being studied.

   FGIs are small; 7–12 individuals take part. Participants are usually homogeneous on an important variable related to the content of the interview (parents of teens at risk for drug use, primary-grade teachers specializing in mathematics). It is an intensive interview of a group. In some instances (e.g., young children), group size may be very small (5–6).

(Continued)

(Continued)

Nominal groups are small with 8–12 individuals being involved. They may be heterogeneous, but do not mix superordinates and subordinates together. Higher-level personnel may stifle the open expression of ideas by those who work for them.

General Rules/Details for the Three Procedures

A person should not be interrupted when speaking.

Points should be made directly and succinctly.

Everyone will be called upon to speak.

Leader jumps in to keep the group moving toward its target since time is limited and also summarizes as relevant what the group has accomplished up to that point.

Some ideas and thoughts may be put in a parking lot for later discussion.

Each group process has unique operational rules that are implemented by the leader, whose role is critical to the success of what the group will generate for the needs assessment.

Arrangements must be made for many little yet need-to-be-attended-to details including:

location (fairly large room for the CGF with breakout rooms if small groups are part of the meeting);

more intimate rooms for FGIs and NGTs;

roundtable setups for the FGIs and NGTs;

formal invitations soliciting attendance;

follow-up procedures for ensuring attendance;

recording procedures (taping, videos, etc.); and

refreshments and so forth.

FGI participants are often paid for their involvement.

All meetings have an agenda; name tags and/or name tents for the smaller groups could be used to allow people to get to know each other.

Selecting Appropriate Leadership

What groups produce is dependent on the skills of the leader. While many can plan a meeting, few have the skills to make the dream a reality.

The leader:

sets a tone that is open and gets people to invest in the process and voice their opinions even if different from those of others;

maintains control and keeps the group moving forward in an engaged way;

appreciates group processes: when to listen, summarize, probe, and tolerate "pregnant pauses" as people are collecting their thoughts;

establishes the right amount of rapport with the group—too little and it may not respond, and too much and it says what will please the leader instead of honest opinions;

must be alert to tabling ideas and when to gently and softly close off responses from those who run on too long or have an ax to grind;

ideally has had such experience before and may even be known in the community for this skill, fairness, and unbiased perspectives; and

should not represent a point of view, especially that of management.

The choice of the right leader cannot be overemphasized. This thought was noted in the "pennywise but pound foolish" example in Chapter 3.

Implementing the Meeting

With preparation completed, hopefully the meeting takes place as planned, but don't be upset if it doesn't. Remember that a meeting is an opportunity to learn new information about the area of need.

Ideas may be generated by groups that the NAC never considered in prior deliberations. That is why groups were a good idea in the first place. Be open to new directions, even to redesigning and retooling the needs assessment strategy and emphasis. This is a healthy outlook to be encouraged.

In many group processes, the goal is to achieve consensus or to see if there is a degree of consensus or coming together of opinion. The leader determines if there is a consensus but must not force (coerce) it.

Reporting on the Meeting and Using the Information Collected

Information gained from good input should be utilized.

Think of how the input will be captured and used. To whom and in what format will it be reported? Could it be used for public relations purposes in the community and organization?

For publicity, a local reporter (in education, health, community development, etc.) could attend the CGF (in particular) to report on what was taking place.

Tape (audio or video) sessions with a person or two acting as roving recorders (especially at the CGF).

Collect all work products from meetings.

As soon as possible after the meeting, staff debrief for immediate impressions. Resist the temptation to unwind and totally relax (do so later).

(Continued)

(Continued)

Describe the atmosphere of the meeting and the main themes that came from it. Independently, each person generates a summary of what occurred, what was missing, and so on. Team members should compare/collate their ideas into a meaningful document regarding session outcomes.

For multiple meetings, prepare a final document across them.

Don't be afraid to change the structure of subsequent meetings after the first one. Insight gained may indicate a shift to a deeper and more probing set of questions as well as a different agenda for the second and third sessions.

   (Kumar & Altschuld, 1999a and b, changed questions after analyzing responses to original field interview questions. Via those changes, they tested their understanding of subtle elements of a project.)

The final report briefly describes the meeting context along with agendas, questions asked, nature of the discussion, and a listing of attendees.

An important part of the report is the patterns that were discerned and work products of the group. What are they, and how do they fit with what was already known about needs? Are they consistent with other data collected in Phases I and II? In what ways do they corroborate and/or not corroborate? The report of the meetings is part of the documentation of the needs assessment project.

Now the fun comes. Go back to Table 4.1 near the beginning of the prior chapter. You could simply include the results from the group procedures in an expanded version of the table.

Lastly, contact the reporter(s) who attended and, if appropriate, share the synopsis of the meetings with that (those) person(s).

Specifics About the Group Processes

Aside from these guidelines, there are some unique dimensions for each group process that should be noted. They are shown in Figure 5.2.

❖   STEP 4: PREPARING FOR
      THE FINAL NAC MEETING OF PHASE II

This final meeting is where crucial needs-related decisions are made. Prepare for it carefully. It may go 3-plus hours depending on the severity of problems identified and what it might take to overcome them. NAC members have been involved throughout the needs assessment

Figure 5.2   Unique Dimensions of Group Processes Used in Needs Assessment

---

Community Group Forums

Not the initial activity in needs assessment, but usually after other data are collected

Prepare early—it takes more lead time than meets the eye

Carefully select a cross-section of individuals who represent key needs assessment constituencies and who will contribute to the meeting

Solicit attendance and be diligent in getting people to the meeting

It is helpful if the leader has experience in working with groups and needs assessment

Think about having small break-out group aspects to the meeting

Coleaders may be needed

Think through the data that will be obtained and their analysis/reporting

Focus Group Interviews

Select participants who are homogeneous on key criteria (faculty for issues related to curriculum, school nurses for child abuse)

Solicit participation (if a few individuals do not show up, results are seriously affected)

Carefully choose the leader so group members will feel free in voicing their opinions with others there

Ask questions requiring description and explanation, not yes/no responses

Start with more general questions and then move to more specific probes (generally FGIs have between 5 and 10 questions)

What have you liked most about your science and mathematics classes in your first year of college?

What have you liked least?

Why did you like or not like these things?

What problems have you encountered in these courses?

What is the nature of those problems?

How have the problems been resolved?

Follow a general pattern as below

Warm-up—people introduce themselves to get used to talking

Explain the nature of the interview, ground rules, and the topic

(Continued)

(Continued)

Go around the group, beginning with the general questions first

Frequently summarize, noting where there is or is not consensus

Ask if summary is accurate

Go through the questioning sequence but move in new directions if responses so indicate

Complete the interview and thank participants

Participants answer a few written demographic questions as a check on sampling

Nominal Group Technique

Steps in an NGT must be followed, especially those where there is no interaction amongst group members

Provide a brief introduction to the topic

State rules, noting that discussion only occurs at the end

Participants silently brainstorm and write down comments for each of the topics or prompts supplied for this purpose

What might be the implications if we did this? (List as many as you can.)

What do you think are the major forces that will affect education in the next 5–10 years? (List all that you are able to.)

Move through the group (a round robin) where each person offers one item from his or her list, which is placed on a board or overhead

Ask and record how many people had similar ideas

Have them cross similar ones off their own list

Proceed until no more ideas are given

Prevent discussion during the collection of ideas

If an idea is not clear, ask the person who generated it to clarify but not to provide a rationale

Clean up things that are not clear

Combine items where possible

Each person individually and silently picks his or her top 5 or 10 items

Collate the rankings or selections

Put in rank order

Conduct a general discussion of the results

The NGT has no interaction until the very last part of the procedure (*it is nominal, a group in name only*)

Table 5.2 Rules for Using Data From Multiple Sources

		Situations	
Need	Situation 1— Data Agree	Situation 2—Data Are in Partial Agreement	Situation 3—Data Do Not Agree or Are Contradictory
1	This is ideal for all data are corroborating the need Present the need emphasizing that all data are complementary	If most sources point toward the same need, the results are still reasonably good If there aren't any sources in disagreement or contradictory in nature, just note that the agreement was based on a smaller set of sources If a disagreeing or noncorroborative source was not as well implemented as other sources, consider disregarding its results If the results are troubling, ask some external individuals (professors, planners, etc.) to look at them and help in dealing with the disagreements Consider collecting more data via interviews, observations, etc.	Worst possible case Simply leave the data as is and let the NAC come to its best possible judgment although this may not be a desirable course to follow Identify the strongest data source in regard to clarity of outcome and strength of implementation, and then its results become the basis for decisions while noting the disagreements Use the last two strategies suggested for Situation 2 with probably the need for the collection of more data being the way to go
2	See above	See above	See above

process, have seen results, and know what has been going on but may not be on an intimate basis with the entire assessment. The first agenda item would be a brief overview of what transpired and to see if NAC members have reviewed reports and materials. Many things could be

Table 5.3   Summarizing Needs Assessment Data From Multiple and Diverse Methods

	Methods		
Need	Surveys	Focus Group Interviews	Records
1	xxxx	ooooo	****
2	xxxx	oo	***
3	xx	oo	****
n	——	——	——

sent in advance of the meeting. Alert the NAC that the following topics will be covered during the meeting:

- a description of the process and progress that has been made;

- a summary of Phase I and Phase II results (here is where the prior work comes into play and where dated tables are valuable);

- a composite table of results across methods (Table 5.2) to guide decisions;

- an initial prioritization of needs; and

- preliminary considerations of what might be causing high-priority needs and possible solution strategies.

❖ STEP 5: THE NAC MEETING

Everything is now ready for the meeting. Since much has to be accomplished, adhere to the schedule with adequate (not overly long) periods allotted for discussion. Start by summarizing what has been done and learned so far. Be comprehensive yet focused. Allow a few minutes for questions and comments. Explain how Table 5.3 (the culmination of the work in Phases I and II) was produced. Briefly describe issues related to it (e.g., where the data are not in concurrence). Ask for input before moving to prioritizing the needs—selecting the small subset to be recommended for further action and use of organizational/other resources (a major point in the needs assessment process).

Prioritization, Causal Analysis, and
Preliminary Consideration of Solutions

Although this seems like more of a Phase III activity, it is here for a reason. Consider how many assessments proceed. Throughout the process, the NAC has dealt with possible causes, solutions, and even priorities before now. The NAC has been capitalizing on the information and understanding gained during the assessment. In prior tables, columns have been included about what might be causing or affecting a need and strategies for resolving problems.

The effort from Phase I up to the present has been honing in on a subset of needs. Priorities, albeit not formal ones, have been established. One small concern is whether we should look at the causes of needs before prioritizing. They undoubtedly influence how we prioritize, so should we prioritize before examining causes and solution strategies? One way to proceed is to determine preliminary priorities in Phase II and then quickly think through possible causes as they relate to potential solution strategies. It is easy in Phase III, as the NAC looks more at causes and solutions, to reevaluate priorities and shift them as necessary.

5.1 Prioritizing Needs

While there are many criteria and methods for prioritizing, keep the procedure simple. Remember that the NAC already has a good sense of needs and their causes. It has a perception of what the organization might face if it doesn't deal with a need. (The need might disappear with the passage of time, the counterfactual state, or might expand and become even more pronounced.)

To determine priorities, establish criteria for NAC members to individually rate need areas. Then determine collective ratings, noting disagreements. Before going to the results in Table 5.3, recognize that the NAC could determine its own categories for rating. Use a straightforward 1–5 (where 5 is highest) rating scale and limit the number of criteria (up to three or four). Criteria might be:

- overall importance to the organization;

- size of the need;

- risk to the organization (political, economic, etc.) if the need was ignored;

- feasibility of the need being resolved by the organization;

- extent to which the data sources agree (if prioritization was limited to needs that had achieved such agreement, this would not be a criterion); and

- willingness of staff members to resolve high-priority needs.

Analyze the ratings as in Figure 5.3. You have to obtain the total and the average ratings for importance, size, and feasibility for each need under scrutiny. Note that Rater 3 has a somewhat different view from others in the group. Since NACs are not large, such differences could be discussed in a tactful manner. If there is real disagreement, there might be a second round of prioritizing for the need(s) in contention. Which needs stand out as priorities? Which ones have high totals with minimal or limited disagreement?

5.2 Causal Analysis of the High-Priority Needs and Potential Solution Strategies

The focus is on the high-priority needs. Other needs, although important, are not of much interest now. They may be reexamined at a later time. For the high-priority needs, what is causing them, and what can be done to rectify the problems? With complex needs in a large organization, it may be necessary to use sophisticated procedures for causal analysis, identifying criteria for possible solutions, and determining what solutions may

Figure 5.3 Summarizing Priority Ratings for Needs

Criteria for Rating					
Need	Rater	Importance	Size	Feasibility	Total
1	1	4	4	5	14
	2	5	4	4	13
	3	3	3	3	9
	4	5	4	5	14
	n	–	–	–	–
Totals					
Average					

involve. But here, let's deal with a basic technique, cause consequence analysis (CCA, described by Witkin & Altschuld, 1995).

In it, prioritized needs are listed as the first column followed by the columns of causes, consequences (what will those causes produce?), "difficulty to correct" (rated from low to high), and criticality (how critical is this cause to the need as rated from 1 to 5?). All causes would be listed for a need even if just educated guesses of the NAC. The NAC might refer back to tables from Phases I and II where potential causes and solutions have been listed. The committee would be encouraged to think of other causes and/or solutions. CCA is depicted in Table 5.4.

Subdivide the NAC so that each subgroup concentrates on certain prioritized needs and pull together these subgroups' thoughts about causality. From there it is a short hop to a discussion of what the criteria for solution strategies could be. Open the discussion and have the NAC brainstorm features it sees as being necessary for the solution to have. This kind of discussion changes the pace of the meeting. Obviously, more intense looks at solutions occur in Phase III.

Starting with prioritization to causal analysis and to beginning considerations about solutions, it might seem that these steps in Phase II require a lot of effort. That may be inaccurate because the needs assessment has been constantly narrowing and decreasing the size of the aperture to take a photograph of a thin slice of the landscape. The NAC will be using a shortened list of needs, and at the end of Phase II the task will be challenging but for a reduced number of needs.

Table 5.4   Cause Consequence Analysis

Prioritized Needs	Causes	Consequences	Difficulty to Correct	Criticality
List needs	List causes	What will cause these problems?	Rate causes from high to low	How critical is this particular cause to the need as rated from 1 to 5?

❖ STEP 6: WRAPPING UP THE PROCESS AND PREPARING FOR PHASE III

6.1 Using Results for Decision Making

The facilitator and several committee members write a short synopsis of what has taken place in the last meeting of Phase II, what needs are initial priorities, their causes, and how they might be resolved. The summary is short, and recommendations should be clear as to next steps. This summary will be conveyed to decision makers.

6.2 Schedule a Meeting With Key Decision Makers

Invite members of the NAC to the meeting as observers and make sure that there is time for them to comment if they wish. The facilitator presents an overview of the needs assessment process and recommendations for Phase III. Provide the decision makers with a few of the key dated tables as well as the recommendations prior to the face-to-face meeting. Engage them in discussing options that could be pursued (see Figure 5.4). Four of them are as follows:

Option 1—move into a full set of Phase III activities but with an emphasis on designing an action plan for the organization to implement for high-priority needs.

Option 2—move to Phase III with further exploration of needs, priorities, solution strategies, and action plans as well as how to evaluate the needs assessment effort itself.

Option 3—based on current knowledge, drop any further activity other than documenting and evaluating the process. There is no compelling case for any need or problem area.

Option 4—move directly to action planning without any other Phase III work being required.

Option 2 is the focus of Phase III, and it might be prudent to add several members to the NAC who are familiar with how things get done inside the organizational context. How might a new program or redirecting resources to different ends be handled? What resistance would be encountered? What are the best ways to involve staff and management, and how should information about new directions be communicated? What incentives could improve chances of success? How strong will management support be—what is the nature of commitment to

Figure 5.4   Postassessment Options

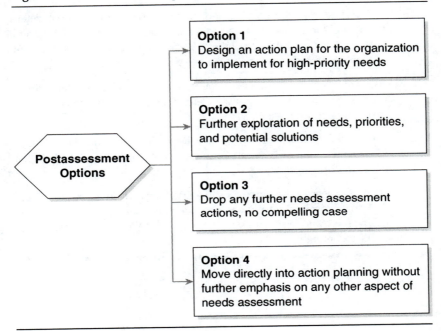

change, innovation, and so forth? These questions require knowledge of how the organization functions and overt and covert barriers. New members also should work well in group and leadership positions and be comfortable with new ideas.

Highlights of the Chapter

The focus of this chapter has been qualitative techniques frequently used in needs assessment; pulling the data together; preliminary prioritization, causal analysis of needs, and consideration of solutions; and presenting results to decision makers. Many assessments employ at least one of the techniques in this chapter, in the previous one, and in the overview in Chapter 2. It is nearly impossible to anticipate every way that needs could be assessed, so other sources should be reviewed beyond what is in this text and KIT.

1. Since Phase II is costly and time consuming to implement, the NAC must strongly feel that more information is warranted based upon what is to be learned.

2. Qualitative and quantitative data together afford a more in-depth picture of needs, and needs assessment budgets should include provisions for both.

3. Qualitative methods require careful planning and preparation effort.

4. The process must be documented to show how priorities were determined and for use in later needs-oriented decisions. Date all tables and keep accurate records of how the NAC accomplished its work. This will also enhance the evaluation of the needs assessment.

5. Assessments generate a large amount of paperwork (tables, summaries, reports, meeting agendas/minutes, etc.) that must be put into a format that aids decision making.

6. Toward the end of Phase II, it may be desirable to include activities (developing solution criteria, posing possible solution strategies) that occur in Phase III.

7. There may seem to be more steps in Phase II than given in Chapters 4 and 5. Actual processes are not cast in stone, with some needs assessments having more and fewer steps, depending on local circumstances. Design yours accordingly.

6

Phase III: Postassessment

❖ INTRODUCTION

In Phase III the focus shifts to translating prioritized needs into plans for the organization. It is the payoff for needs assessment. Decisions are made in regard to services for Level 1 and what Levels 2 and 3 must do to support clients and consumers. How the organization goes about its business will be affected. Jobs and responsibilities (Level 2 in particular) may be restructured or even lost due to redirected priorities. Retraining may be required, and work might have to be performed in different ways from what individuals know or have experienced before. A new area or emphasis will demand resources (human, fiscal, attention of management, etc.). Clearly, needs assessment is a mechanism by which organizations change, develop, and learn.

Phase III might be contentious. Change and growth can be exhilarating but are not always easy and come with costs and benefits. The facilitator and the needs assessment committee (NAC) must be aware of this and handle it sensitively. This phase, while exciting, must be entered cautiously and carefully.

❖ STEP 1: RECONFIGURING THE NAC AND ITS FIRST MEETING: ATTENDING TO OLD BUSINESS

1.1 Examine NAC Membership

It may be desirable as noted previously to reconstitute the NAC with several managers from the organization. They should understand how things get done and not be so wedded to tradition as to look askance at new approaches and ways to view issues. Once selected, enlarge the NAC, or if a few existing members exit, just substitute for them. Keep the rest of the committee intact as harmony, trust, and historical perspective must be maintained.

The facilitator at this point is attentive to nuances, how to explain the need for new members, and how to accomplish the change. An external facilitator should suggest that as Phase III progresses it is better if NAC leadership is less outsider led. The facilitator should stay on as an advisor for what is now an internal action-oriented committee.

1.2 The First Phase III Meeting of the NAC

Since there are new members, review what has been done and ask the NAC whether it is comfortable moving into identifying, selecting, or devising solution strategies. Use prior summaries and tables to get everyone on the same page. The following questions would guide the group:

- Looking at Phases I and II, are you satisfied that there is a firm basis for the prioritized needs?

- Is there a solid grasp of Level 1 discrepancies, their nature, and what might be causing them?

- Is enough known about Levels 2 and 3 to proceed into the solution-oriented part of the work?

- Do we have adequate information about issues and concerns associated with these levels to determine important criteria for existing solutions and/or developing new ones?

- Are you so sick of the problem/analysis emphasis that you just have to get to something else?

Assuming that most answers are yes, the NAC generates criteria for solutions. If many responses are no, engage in more formal prioritization and causal analysis or seek out more information particularly for Levels 2 and 3. Let's for a moment consider the *no* answers. For them, use Sork's (1998) procedure for prioritizing or try alternative causal analysis procedures (fishbone diagrams, fault tree analysis). If necessary, go back to parts of Phases I and II (see Figure 6.1).

1.3 The Sork (1998) Procedure

Each need is rated on five importance and three feasibility criteria. The criteria could be differentially weighted, but generally equal, whole number (1.0) weights are used. The five importance criteria are (a) number of people affected, (b) contribution to the mission of the organization (needs assessments must fit organizational missions and the Level 1 clientele served), (c) the degree to which the need demands immediate attention, (d) the magnitude of the discrepancy, and (e) instrumental value. The last criterion refers to a solution strategy that has a positive impact on multiple needs (a "statin" drug that lowers both cholesterol and blood pressure demonstrates instrumental value). High instrumental value is important for prioritizing needs.

Other criteria could be added by the NAC. Think of the risk of not attending to a need or the likelihood that it will be resolved in ways not requiring any action (public transportation riders increase as gas prices rise, reducing the demand for costly fuel and prompting calls for cheaper transportation—bikes, motor scooters, etc.). Even consider how politics might affect prioritization (see Example 6.1).

Example 6.1

Examining Those Doctoral Programs

Doctoral programs are facing increased pressure to look at themselves and move in new directions. What should be the nature of content and training? What should be added or dropped? What might fields look like in 10 years? How do they cope with the challenges graduates will face?

A foundation created a project that encouraged selected areas in universities to become part of a study of these programs. The institutions did not receive much support to do this with resources coming from internal funds in a time of budgetary pressure.

Why would universities participate without sufficient external dollars being there? A sincere desire to improve would be one reason. On the other hand, the national group behind the effort is well known and prestigious. Its movers and shakers are prominent and respected in educational circles.

Figure 6.1 Initial Reflection in Phase III

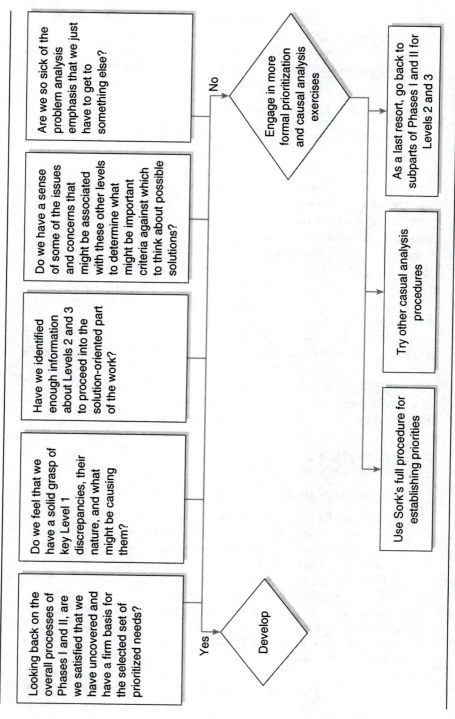

One could speculate that the political press (risk) may have outweighed financial considerations in the decision. Could there be a political backlash to not being involved? Could major universities afford to not participate? Political issues do exert pressure on decisions.

Returning to Sork (1998), Tables 6.1a and 6.1b depict assessment of the five importance and three feasibility criteria. A sequential approach is advocated. Needs are separated from solutions as much as possible. Importance is more related to the former and feasibility to the latter. The NAC should first rate importance followed by feasibility. In this manner, if there were 10 need areas and 3 were most important, only those 3 would be examined in terms of feasibility. The goal is to select the needs of most importance that could be feasibly resolved but not to confound the two when prioritizing. Each person independently rates the two categories with importance being considered first. In Table 6.1a, Need Area 2 was more highly rated for importance and feasibility than the other need.

1.4 More Causal Analysis If Needed

Still dealing with the *no* side of the answers, additional causal analysis may be required especially if the problem is complex. One recommendation would be to use qualitative fault tree analysis (FTA) for which the NAC identifies a failure or an undesirable event (UE) for the need of concern and specifies factors that may cause the UE to occur. From there the group creates a fault tree with the UE at the top with possible causes leading up to it. Figure 6.2 is a qualitative fault tree for a wellness project that would help employees of a national moving company avoid or reduce the occurrence of back problems. Failure comes from either inadequate program design or low motivation to participate.

Before constructing the tree, the NAC proposes and collates potential causes, eliminates duplicates, and sorts them into main ones and subcauses contributing to the main ones. Usually three to four iterations of a tree are required. Causes are separated into those that can be affected by the organization and those that are external to it or not amenable to its influence. Why deal with the latter, particularly if they are strong? The NAC has to consider if the organization can resolve the need or if it can change external causes to its advantage.

The fault tree diagram in Figure 6.2 has additional features. There are "and" and "or" gates. "And" gates signify that all of the lower events leading to a higher cause (going up the tree) have to occur together to bring about the higher one. They are preferred because it is

Table 6.1 Sork's (1998) Prioritizing Strategy

6.1a Importance Criteria (criteria weighted equally)

Need Area	# Affected	Contribution to Organization	Immediate Attention	Instrumental Value	Size of Discrepancy	Sum of Means	
1	3.5*	3.9	2.7	3.2	3.6	16.9	Lower rank
2	3.9	4.2	3.8	4.1	4.2	19.2	Higher rank
3							
N							

*The numbers in the cells are averages of 1–5 ratings given by individual group members.

6.1b Feasibility Criteria (criteria weighted equally)

Need Area	Educational Efficacy	Resource Availability	Commitment to Change	Sum of Means	Final Rank
1	2.7	3.6	2.9	9.2	Lower
2	3.4	3.9	4.1	11.4	Higher
3					
N					

*The numbers in the cells are averages of 1–5 ratings given by individual group members.

Note: Date these tables and other pertinent work products as part of the chronological record of accomplishments.

Figure 6.2   Two Branches of a Fault Tree for the Moving Company Wellness
Program

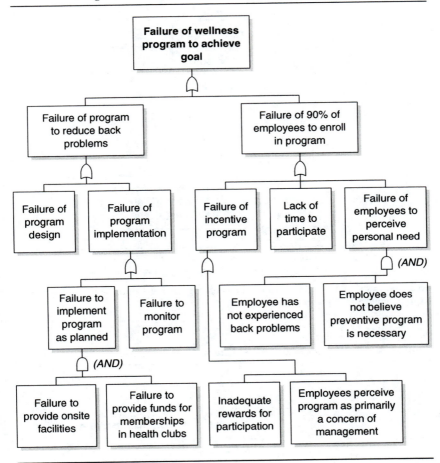

Source: From *Planning and Conducting Needs Assessments: A Practical Guide,* by B. R. Witkin
and J. W. Altschuld, 1995, Thousand Oaks, CA: Sage. Used with permission.

less probable that all of the lower causes will jointly take place to bring
about the higher cause. "Or" gates are not desirable. They denote that
only one (not all) of the lower causes has to take place for the higher
one to become a reality. Such gates are seen in Figures 6.3 and 6.4.

Fault trees can be quantified to identify the most likely path to failure, but the process takes time and is warranted only for complicated
needs. Lastly, there is another use of FTA pertinent to needs assessment
and program planning. FTA can determine in advance how a selected

Figure 6.3   Illustration of an "Or" Gate

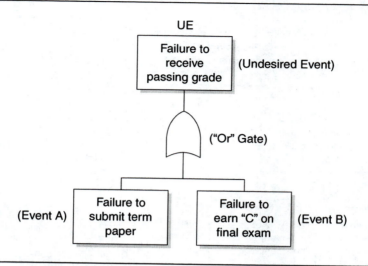

Source: From *Planning and Conducting Needs Assessments: A Practical Guide,* by B. R. Witkin and J. W. Altschuld, 1995, Thousand Oaks, CA: Sage. Used with permission.

Note: The undesired event (UE) could be caused by either Event A or Event B if both requirements are mandatory.

Figure 6.4   Illustration of an "And" Gate

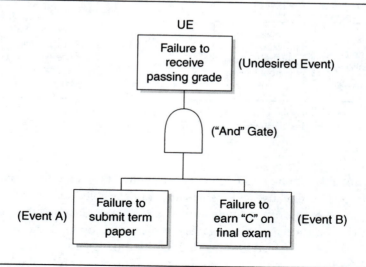

Source: From *Planning and Conducting Needs Assessments: A Practical Guide,* by B. R. Witkin and J. W. Altschuld, 1995, Thousand Oaks, CA: Sage. Used with permission.

Note: The undesired event (UE) could occur only if both Event A and Event B occur, if the events are alternative options.

solution strategy might possibly fail. In other words, it can help to ascertain causes of a need or the weak links in a solution.

There is more complexity to FTA than appears at first glance with the goal here being to explain the approach but not go into all the details. A qualitative fault tree is heuristic and can be constructed in a fairly short time. It has value for formative evaluation and the identification of key process variables. Other causal analysis techniques such as the fishbone diagram (Witkin & Altschuld, 1995, and Book 3 in this KIT) may be used, but FTA is good for complex needs because it reveals causal pathways to failure and how to prevent them from occurring. Let's move to *yes* answers to the earlier questions.

❖ STEP 2: THE FIRST NAC MEETING: ATTENDING TO *NEW* BUSINESS

2.1 Criteria for Solutions

There are five main ways to select solutions for needs (Altschuld & Witkin, 2000): reviewing the literature, benchmarking, multi-attribute utility theory (MAUT), simple multi-attribute rating technique (SMART), and quality function deployment (QFD). Generating criteria for solutions is the first step in the process. The NAC must think about what should be in a solution. It might look at the "parking lot" of ideas and possibilities for solutions from Phases I and II.

What features of a solution will make it work in our situation? What kinds of new or changed skills on the part of staff might be required? How long might a startup period be? What are the short-term and long-term outcomes? How much will it cost to begin the solution, bring it up to a satisfactory level of performance, and maintain a high quality of delivery/implementation? How will different solutions affect the problem?

The NAC should examine prior needs assessment work before the first meeting in this phase and come to it with suggestions. Send the committee probes such as above and ask what would be in an ideal solution and what would be in one that is less than ideal. What makes for a good strategy that would work for us? Aside from Level 1, how would it affect Levels 2 and 3? NAC members provide entries for a table based on relevant columns from their ideas. At the actual meeting:

- discuss criteria for choosing solutions;

- record the criteria (separated by the three levels if appropriate); and

- divide the NAC into teams to seek more information on proposed solutions.

2.2 In the Interim From the First to the Second Meeting

Solutions might be derived from "scratch," but usually that is not the starting point. Much information can be found in the literature (some members could work with a local librarian to see what is there). Others might conduct interviews with individuals who have insight into the problem and potential solutions. During the period between the first and second meetings of the NAC, the facilitator takes the information being generated and develops a table to capture it. The facilitator requests that the teams provide short descriptions of solutions and brief commentary as to how well each satisfies the criteria. The purpose is not advocacy but to help in analyzing what each solution has to offer. The scenario format from the Program Evaluation Kit (Herman, Morris, & Fitz-Gibbon, 1987) might be borrowed. It puts a solution into concrete focus (see Figure 6.5).

A summary of what is being learned in table format (Table 6.2) should be sent about a week before the next meeting or at least be ready for it. The scenarios could accompany the table with a few pages of text.

❖ STEP 3: THE SECOND MEETING OF THE NAC

3.1 The Solution Strategies

The NAC reviews solutions against criteria—are some better, or would some better appeal to and be acceptable to the organization and its staff? Is there enough there to choose a solution that all see as useful for the organization? What kinds of tough questions might be asked about our choice? The meeting may be spirited, and it is OK if

Figure 6.5   Preliminary Solution Description to Be Used by NAC Members

Solution	Level 1 Participants would be doing	Level 2 Participants would be doing	Level 3 activities
1			
2			

Table 6.2   Format for a Summary Comparing Solution Strategies

Criteria	Solution 1	Solution 2	Solution 3	Solution n
Populations served				
Staff training required				
Key features: 1. 2. 3. 4.				
Startup costs				
Continuation and/or maintenance costs				
Fit with our situation				
Exemplar (site) experience				
Advantages				
Disadvantages				
Will the solution have a positive effect on other problems?				
Could the solution have a negative effect on the situation?				
Other unique features				

the NAC splits in affinity for several strategies. If more information is required before deciding, the NAC continues to collect input for the next meeting.

3.2 The Process Continues Toward a Selection Decision

Keep going until the NAC comes to consensus. Several choices may still be equivalent for there are multiple ways to resolve a problem/need. Report this to the decision makers or go to a more sophisticated way of choosing a solution.

One of the five methods cited before was MAUT. It is attributed to Benjamin Franklin and can easily be applied here. For MAUT:

- You must have two or more solutions to compare.

- Identify 8–10 criteria for judging solutions. You already have criteria in Table 6.2, but there are too many for MAUT. Come to quick agreement as to which ones stand out. MAUT reduces the number even further.

- The NAC *ranks* the criteria in order of importance.

- Proceed through steps that preserve ratios and normalize the weights of those ratios for important criteria—steps that appear more intimidating than they really are (see Figure 6.6).

- Rate each solution in terms of how well it satisfies the weighted criteria.

How MAUT Works

Suppose solutions are needed to reduce the high rate of science teacher turnover in the first 5 years of teaching in inner city schools. The gap is clear, and not attending to it has serious consequences for the teaching force, teacher training institutions, the quality of science education received by students, participation of minorities in the labor

Figure 6.6 Multi-Attribute Utility Theory Application and Criteria

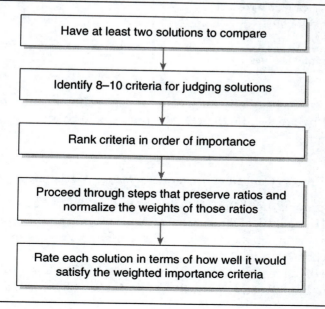

force, and the society that will have disenfranchised individuals and/
or groups.

Solutions are mentoring a beginning teacher by an experienced one
in the same school who is in science (Option 1); mentoring by an out-
standing teacher in the school who is not in science (Option 2); a group
mentoring approach in a school (Option 3); districtwide meetings and
training workshops (Option 4); and a chat room and Internet-based
system with instantaneous assistance (Option 5). Which of these might
be best for the district? (Combining options comes up later.)

First, the NAC specifies criteria upon which to judge the options.
They might be rapidity of contact when there is a problem, degree of
direct human interaction, costs, relevance of assistance to the subject
matter being taught, greater in-depth exposure to teaching techniques,
access to help in resolving problems, and freedom to talk about problems independent of others in the school district (novice teachers may
be reluctant to discuss issues for that would expose weaknesses especially prior to permanent certification).

Each member of the NAC rates the criteria (1 is high, and 5 is low),
and the average ratings are determined. Results are shown below.

Criteria	Average Rating	Ratio	Normalized Weight
Human contact	1.4	80	20
Rapidity	1.8	60	18
Freedom to talk	2.1	58	18
Cost	2.3	55	17
Relevance to subject	2.9	30	9
In-depth exposure	3.4	15	4.5
Other	3.9	10	3

The ratio value comes from giving the lowest-rated criterion an
arbitrary value of 10 and then *judging* that the next ranked criterion is
1.5 times (a ratio) as important, the next is 3 times as important, and
so forth. Each higher criterion is a ratio of the value of 10 (the idea of
preserving ratios).

Sum the ratios (328 in this case), divide the sum into each individual
ratio, and multiply by 100. Notice what happens: Criteria with higher
weights now number four. We could renormalize the four criteria (their

weights total to 73, so the first criterion gets a new normalized weight of $20/73 \times 100$, which equals 27).

MAUT is a good way to make a decision and is a version of the Pareto (Mathison, 2004) principle: If many things can cause a problem, only a small number of them really will. Another example of the principle is that in a large meeting only a small number of people do most of the talking. The principle pares down the criteria to a lesser number that are most important.

Now prepare a MAUT table (Table 6.3). Each option is examined in terms of the smaller set of criteria and assigned (through discussion or averaging of values given by group members) a probability that it will fulfill each criterion, which in turn is multiplied by the normalized weight. The products per option are totaled with the highest total having the greatest potential for resolving the need. Multiple options are necessary for MAUT, and by identifying and looking at them we become more analytical in thinking about the resolution of needs.

Option 5 was given low probabilities for all criteria except freedom to talk. Given this, combining several solution strategies becomes a possibility. MAUT, by forcing us to spell out criteria and explore each option against them, might lead to doing this. (The other two techniques for selecting solutions, SMART and QFD, are more complex and appear less often in needs assessment. See Altschuld & Witkin, 2000.)

Table 6.3   An Example of the Application of MAUT

Criteria (normalized weight)	Option 1	Option 2	Option 3	Option 4	Option 5
Human contact (27)	.8 (.8 × 27)	.75 (.75 × 27)	.7 (.7 × 27)	.65 (.65 × 27)	.4 (.4 × 27)
Rapidity (25)	.8 (.8 × 25)	.75	.8	.4	.65
Freedom (25)	.3	.4	.25	.35	.8
Cost (23)	—	—	—	—	—
Sum of products*					

*Probabilities × normalized weight products are totaled down the column for each option. The option attaining the highest total is the most likely solution for the need.

❖ STEP 4: BENCHMARKING

4.1 Identifying Key Sites to See

So far, most understanding of solutions comes from literature or word of mouth (testimonials). There is no substitute for seeing first-hand how similar needs are being handled by other organizations. Sites could be like your organization or even be in different sectors (public or private) with different foci, but they have been successful in implementing a new approach (quality improvement, intensive staff development, and retooling efforts). Site visits are invaluable for learning about how solutions are being implemented—how other sites did it, impediments, hidden problems that are not talked about (but there), guidance that site personnel could provide, and covert resources that are really necessary for positive results.

Frequently in education, social service, community development, government institutions, the medical community, and businesses, solutions don't transfer well. It is hard to ferret out the under-the surface aspects of programs and projects, the nature of driving personalities, and infrastructure. Without understanding such factors, solutions may fail or be less than optimal when tried at your site. Hopefully, the initial needs assessment budget had funds for small teams to visit exemplary sites. Choose four to five candidates and call them with questions such as above, the length of time a solution has been in operation, how the site dealt with personnel changes, and so forth.

Indicate that a team from your organization will be visiting several locations and ask whether the sites would be amenable to hosting a visit. Contact them with your final decision and thank them, if not visited, for providing input.

4.2 What Should You Look For?

Go back to Tables 6.2 and 6.3 for what to explore onsite. These are more formal things, not the informal ones that are variable from site to site. It is often the *je ne sais quoi* qualities that make programs work. From Altschuld and Witkin (2000), here are some areas for the visitation team to probe into:

How did other sites determine their needs, and how similar are those to yours?

How did they go about the process of change (reorganizing and/or hiring staff, shifting resources in new or different ways, rethinking administrative structure, determining the startup time required, etc.)?

What kinds of incentives were used to increase the likelihood of success?

What would they do differently now based upon what they have learned?

What does it take to maintain the solution strategy?

Has evidence been collected as to whether the need has been resolved?

Have there been any instrumental effects?

What has not worked, and why?

How did they evaluate and/or document what resulted from the solution?

When personnel changed, how was the solution affected?

How is the solution supported?

If they had less money, what would they change?

If they had more, what would they strengthen?

What is the administrative view of the solution, and how does it compare to that of the staff and recipients of services?

Before the visit, the team should be clear about its questions. Onsite, its members separate to take maximum advantage of their time. They should meet daily to discuss and compare insights and perceptions.

When the visit is completed, the host organization is debriefed, using the views that emerged from the team. Site personnel are thanked, and as quickly as possible the team writes a brief summary (under 10 pages) of the highlights and major findings of the visit. It is important that team members be sensitive to the variables that make or break programs. The summaries are shared with the full NAC at its next meeting. They might contain team membership, date/length of the visit and its purposes, short description(s) of observations, main questions asked and content learned in regard to them, what we can use in our situation, what should be avoided, other observations, and recommendations.

❖   STEP 5: ONE MORE NAC MEETING

This meeting is important because the NAC is ready to propose one or several solutions for the highest-priority organizational needs. A sound rationale has to be provided to propel the effort forward and establish clarity for decision makers and staff. They have to understand solutions, implications for the future, and why the organization should adopt what is being recommended.

The NAC reviews information and plans its presentation. It might contain:

- a brief, one-page overview of the needs assessment process;

- highlighted needs that were identified in priority order including the criteria used to sort the needs (Sork's, 1998, importance and feasibility criteria);

- an overview of strategies taken to identify potential solutions for needs;

- the solution most likely to resolve problems and that best fits the organization;

- a summary of what was learned from the benchmarking activity;

- recommendations for developing action plans;

- ways to communicate new directions for review and input with enough time for organizational personnel to consider what has been recommended; and

- a schedule for completing Phase III through action planning and initial tryout.

Many previous tables could be used for the presentation to focus attention on solution strategies (Figure 6.7). The figure has the top parts of some key tables from the needs assessment. It shows a progression from the broad start to a narrow set of prioritized needs. Many variations of the figure are possible depending on your specific situation.

The NAC identifies who does the presentation. Aside from the facilitator, the NAC now has original members augmented by a few managers and/or administrators. It might not be wise to use the latter as presenters. Needs assessment is a highly political act that could upset delicate balances in an organization. Managers might be seen as having vested interests and turf to defend, and the good work of the NAC may go for naught, due not to quality but to views held within the organization. Therefore, the facilitator and a few other NAC members should offer their case for the future relative to prioritized needs.

Figure 6.7 Using Some Key Dated Tables for Communication About the Needs Assessment Process

Table 3.1 One Useful Format for Displaying the Initial Needs Assessment Work   Date: June 1

Area of Concern	What Should Be	What Is	Sources of Information	What We'd Like to Know	Sources of Information
Area 1 Subareas	Standards, expectations	Current status	Records, archives	More about status, perceptions of status, etc.	Other records, interviews, etc.

Initial focusing results

Table 4.1 Focusing on Phase II Activities   Date: July 10

Area of Concern	What We Know	More Knowledge Desirable	Causal Analysis	Possible Solution Criteria	Possible Solutions
Area 1 Subarea 1	Level 1 Level 2 Level 3				

Collecting more information to narrow the focus

in the needs assessment process

Increasing specificity and focus

Table 6.1a Importance Criteria

Need Area	# Affected	Contribution to Organization	Immediate Attention	Instrumental Value	Size of Discrepancy	Sum of Means
1	3.5*	3.9	2.7	3.2	3.6	16.9

Prioritizing based on importance, also do same thing for feasibility

Table 6.2 Format for a Summary Comparing Solution Strategies   Date: September 20

Criteria	Solution 1	Solution 2	Solution 3	Solution n
Population served				

Contrasting solution strategies

Table 6.3 An Example of the Application of MAUT   Date: October 20

Criteria (normalized weight)	Option 1	Option 2	Option 3	Option 4	Option 5
Human contact (27)	.8 (.8 x 27)	.75 (.75 x 27)	.7 (.7 x 27)	.65 (.65 x 27)	.4 (.4 x 27)

Selecting most likely solution

Increasing specificity and focus
in the needs assessment process

133

If the organization decides to move forward, the managers will be prominent in designing action plans to make solutions a reality. They would generate a plan for a full implementation of the solution or one for a pilot test to eliminate bugs before going to widespread organizational use (more on pilot testing shortly).

There are a few more details prior to going public with findings. One is how to get widespread feedback on the findings and proposed solutions in addition to the feedback of the decision makers. Short synopses of results could be distributed, with the NAC scheduling smaller, informal meetings to show what has been done and solicit suggestions, thoughts, and input. Such a mechanism was used by a committee developing and putting in place a standard personnel evaluation procedure in a college where only varied and sporadic procedures had been used before.

In the meetings, the NAC explained how it went about the needs assessment, and the atmosphere was quite open in nature to ease uncertainties about what was being proposed. Without this stance, there may have been strong resistance in the college. Potential problems in implementation were reduced by going directly to those to be served or who had to deal with the change.

Another concern was the costs of the recommendations. Certainly from Tables 6.2 and 6.3, there is a sense of what changes might cost, but concrete budgets are required. This is why an expanded NAC (adding several managers) was advocated for Phase III. A way to estimate costs would be through pilot testing new procedures. This helps to see who would be involved in full implementation, how long it would take, what kinds of outcomes are to be expected, who will be responsible for the project, how the effort should be evaluated, what types of variables should be measured, and how data will be used. The costs of this smaller effort (people involved, time required including allowance for snags, materials, equipment) can be extrapolated to the entire organization. Start small while thinking big.

A test would have been worthwhile for the personnel evaluation system mentioned above. Concerns from staff arose about the system (ratings on performance forms, position descriptions that had not been updated, feedback from external individuals who best knew the nature of some jobs, and 360-degree evaluation of supervisors). Since change can be disruptive, tryouts on a smaller scale are warranted and make good sense.

If the NAC is satisfied as to where it is, schedule meetings with the decision makers and staff. The needs assessment is rapidly moving toward its final activities.

❖ STEP 6: THE DISSEMINATION MEETINGS

The facilitator takes the lead at meetings with support from the NAC. Describe the assessment process and findings and stress the importance and feasibility criteria of Sork (1998). By explaining procedures, the credibility of the process is demonstrated. It might be wise to note needs of high priority that were not selected due to such factors as the following:

- Underlying causes cannot be resolved beyond the influence of the organization.

- Some needs may be important, but lesser numbers of individuals are affected.

- There may be more willingness in the organization to tackle certain problems.

The NAC is an advisory group. Decisions reside in the formal structure of the organization. Throughout the needs assessment, the NAC frequently communicates what it has been doing; thus there are not many surprises. The presentations are a culmination of what has been a forward-thinking endeavor sponsored by the organization to better serve and/or to provide useful products to those with needs. Questions will be raised, and there will be inquiries about budgets, but the NAC has done its homework. It should be able to deal with such concerns while acknowledging where it had less information than desired.

Everyone has reviewed the report and recommendations of the NAC and endorsed moving into planning and implementing that strategy. The work has paid off, so celebrate a job that has been performed to a high standard of quality. Go out as a group and have an ice cream or a libation to let off steam!

❖ STEP 7: THE ACTION PLAN—THE SUCCESS MAP

7.1 Internal NAC Leadership

An external facilitator is needed for guidance, evaluation of the needs assessment process, and documentation of what has transpired, but designing and implementing solutions rests on the inspiration, commitment, drive, and creativity of those who make them come to life. The NAC picks new leadership or at least suggests who would be good in the role. This is important because the NAC continues and a new leader must be able to work with it.

7.2 Creating the Success Map

The committee should produce a success map (program plan, logic map) for a full implementation or a pilot test of the solution. The NAC has most of the ingredients for the plan—underlying causes, needs at the three levels, literature review, benchmarking, and much more information.

How specific should the map be? From one stance, the devil is in the details, so make it specific, laying out every aspect of the projected endeavor. In the evaluation literature there are "logic maps" that are quite minute in detail. They are useful for thinking about solutions and spotting flaws in programs but may be too much. Groups can become so enmeshed in the pieces that they lose sight of the total picture or details may appear overwhelming.

We recommend a more general type of success map, one that fits on a page or so and gives an overall sense of meaning. A simple visual is better for establishing common perceptions of what will be happening. Two examples (Figures 6.8 and 6.9) illustrate the idea. Figure 6.8 is a general roadmap, from start to finish, for the college performance management system.

The committee had done a needs assessment over 6 months and derived criteria for potential solutions (up-to-date position descriptions, multiple sources of feedback from internal and external observers of an individual's work, inclusion of opportunities for enhancing skills). The NAC conducted a search of the literature for solutions that fit the local situation and how the best features of them might be combined.

With a solution in hand, a first-year limited tryout of the overall system (there were some 400 personnel to be evaluated in 20 units) was conducted. Full implementation was planned for the following 3 years. The purpose of the pilot test was to learn about bugs in the system and evaluate it as to what was working and disruptions caused by the new procedures.

In Figure 6.8, there are four elements to the system (developing written materials; developing training procedures for using the new system; maintaining regular communication with staff, administrators, and faculty; and evaluating the process). The diagram shows the full effort in an easily communicated manner. The evaluation was only partially carried out due to a change of leadership, but it is noteworthy that the system is still used in the college (12 years later) with minor modifications.

Figure 6.8 Success Map for First Tryout of Performance Management System

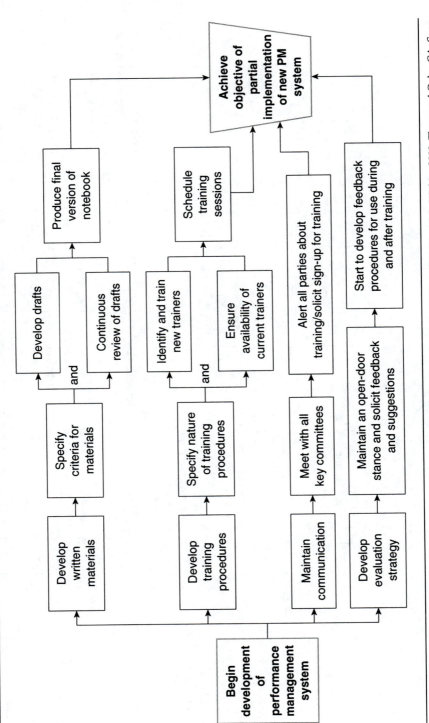

Source: From *From Needs Assessment to Action: Transforming Needs Into Solution Strategies*, by J. W. Altschuld and B. Witkin, 2000, Thousand Oaks, CA: Sage. Used with permission.

Figure 6.9 Rudimentary Success Map for a Program Designed to Reduce the Back Problems of Employees of a Nationwide Moving Company

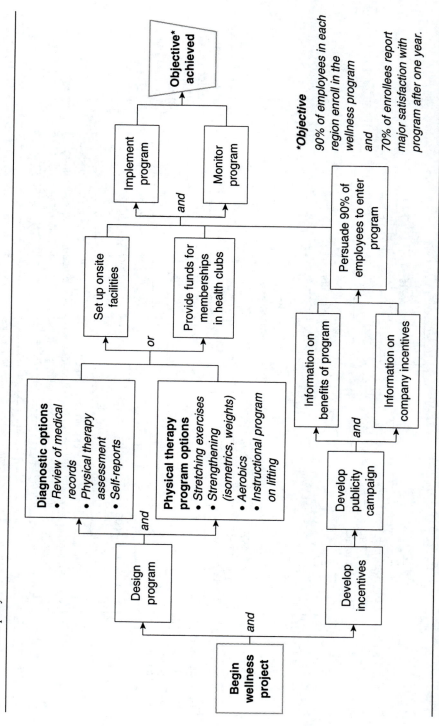

Source: From *Planning and Conducting Needs Assessments: A Practical Guide,* by B. R. Witkin and J. W. Altschuld, 1995, Thousand Oaks, CA: Sage. Used with permission.

Another example is in Figure 6.9. The figure is for the moving company health project (see Figure 6.1). It too is a simple picture of that project. When Figures 6.1 and 6.7 are compared, various parts of the needs assessment process can be used in tandem to produce impressive results. The NAC has identified solutions, criteria for them, outcomes to be expected, and possible causes of failure. The processes are interrelated, and the NAC considers them almost simultaneously.

They are the juxtaposition of a success map and the analysis of the causes of how a solution might fail. The first map shows two pathways for the health program to be implemented—developmental activities and those designed to attract enrollment and full engagement in the program. Causal analysis through FTA (Figure 6.2) suggests that the success might be in jeopardy due to motivational factors. If the tree had been quantified (estimating the probabilities of causes and the degree to which they contribute to a higher tree cause), it is likely that failure would occur more through the motivational side of the project.

7.3 Force Field Analysis

Planning for change also relates to organizational forces that support or oppose it. Opposition may be overt or subtle and result in less-than-optimum success of a solution. The NAC identifies forces in favor of and against the solution. The issue is to strengthen and lessen the positive and negative ones, respectively. In Figure 6.10, forces for or against an entity are in balance; in Figure 6.11, the strength of forces is indicated by the length of the arrow shaft.

What happens in a solution is that an organization seeks a new state of equilibrium. Forces (groups and individuals) not aligned with the change may work against or perhaps even kill it with benign avoidance. Some may be vociferous in opposition or quietly strive to defuse (defeat) the change. Individuals or groups may not commit to altering what they are used to, or they may give the appearance of commitment. Conversely, others sincerely back the innovation as a way to improve the organization. Some may commit because they gain advantage. Whatever the case, the NAC determines how to sell the change and make it a reality. How are negative and positive forces taken into account?

1. The NAC identifies forces (administrative support or lack thereof, individual enthusiasm or antipathy, sustainable budgetary resources, quality of the innovation) that affect success or failure.

Figure 6.10   Generic Diagram for Force Field Analysis: Driving and
                   Restraining Forces

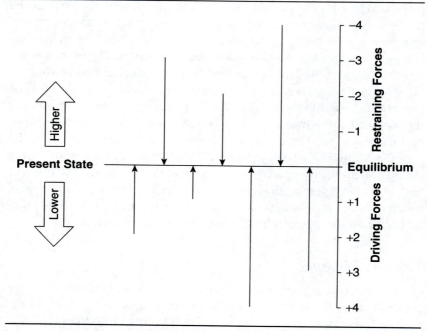

Source: From *Planning and Conducting Needs Assessments: A Practical Guide*, by B. R. Witkin and J. W. Altschuld, 1995, Thousand Oaks, CA: Sage. Used with permission.

2. It estimates the strength of forces, disregarding whether they are negative or positive. A force may be positive and negative (some administrators are in favor, and others are not).

3. Array the forces around an equilibrium line representing the innovation with some impeding and others facilitating it. Use arrows to denote the impact (strength of each source).

4. Review the force field diagram and decide how to increase positive forces and lessen negative ones.

❖ STEPS 8 AND 9: EVALUATION OF THE SOLUTION
   STRATEGY AND OF THE NEEDS ASSESSMENT ITSELF

8.1 Evaluation of the Action Plan

Previous needs assessment activities are useful for evaluation of the action plan. This is especially true of the criteria for solution strategies and causal analysis. They point to what should be in formative/summative

Figure 6.11 Force Field Analysis of Catalog Recommendation in a Purchasing Directors' Agency

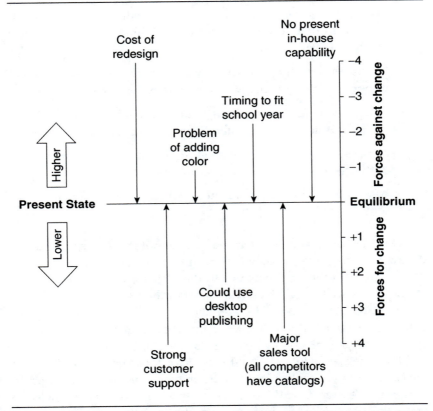

Source: From *Planning and Conducting Needs Assessments: A Practical Guide*, by B. R. Witkin and J. W. Altschuld, 1995, Thousand Oaks, CA: Sage. Used with permission.

evaluation. The FTA for the moving van company is a good illustration. The criteria for success were part of it as was the most likely path to failure of the project if implemented. Thus, outcomes to be measured and areas for formative evaluation are clearer.

Beyond what and where to assess, the NAC has been reviewing literature, interviewing experts, and visiting sites. These activities add to the evaluative understandings of the NAC. Now, how should the *needs assessment itself* be evaluated?

8.2 Evaluation of the Needs Assessment Process

The literature seldom contains evaluations of needs assessments. Possible reasons are:

- Many assessments have been only partially utilized, and reporting on same would relate to a less-than-positive outcome.

- Insufficient resources are available for evaluation since assessments are often done on a shoestring (let alone with the expense of evaluation).

- Needs assessment requires a serious investment of time and human resources with little energy and motivation left for evaluation.

- The process has been evaluated but for organizational purposes, not for publication (the evaluations are buried in a file drawer).

- There is not a good stepwise set of procedures for capturing all of the needs assessment process and its nuances.

- Also, if the entire effort was not well done, it might be burdensome to evaluate it.

One idea for evaluation stressed throughout the KIT is that all key documents and tables be dated. They are a record of how needs were dealt with from the first meetings to the plan for action. Tables done this way (Figure 6.7) will be a major part of the final report submitted by the NAC (Appendix). All materials (tables, forms, records, instruments, site visit reports) should be archived electronically and for referral when the organization reassesses its needs as it ultimately will!

The external facilitator could conduct a focus group interview of the NAC with the results placed in the archive. This interview could be part of a reception after the needs assessment is over to acknowledge and celebrate the NAC. Include with the invitation the final needs assessment report for review. Interview questions might include the following:

- Reflecting on the needs assessment process, what stands out to you as most positive?

- What stands out as the less than positive?

- What kinds of changes would you make if we do this again?

- Are there ways in which we could have speeded up the process?

- What are your honest impressions of how successful we have been?

- Are there other perceptions that would be useful to this discussion?

The Needs Assessment Process Is Now Done!

Highlights of the Chapter

There were more details of the process for Phase III than in Chapter 2 (Table 2.2). In Phase III the NAC may more formally conduct some aspects of needs assessment (prioritizing, analyzing causes) from Phase II. The NAC might be reconfigured, and benchmarking visits might be conducted. Keep the following thoughts in mind for Phase III:

1. The NAC must reexamine where it is before developing action plans. Is there enough information to proceed to planning? If not, go back a few paces before advancing.

2. Phase III moves into criteria for and locating and finding possible solutions.

3. The NAC determines the solution most likely to resolve the needs-based problem(s).

4. The NAC frames and presents arguments for the solutions to be presented to the organization. Pilot test them before going to full implementation.

5. When examining solutions, look at how they were evaluated—what variables were measured, what design was used, what were the results of the evaluation, and so forth. Note: Causal analysis suggests key foci for the evaluation.

6. Evaluation of the needs assessment itself is important. Has the work of the group been organized into a good historical record? Are all tables and work products dated? Is everything stored and accessible so that subsequent activities like this one will not have to start over when the organization again decides to delve into its needs?

7. After the assessment is over, debrief the NAC about what went right or wrong, the success of the effort, what it would do differently, whether the process could be shortened without loss of quality, and so forth. This will make for a better needs assessment the next time around.

Appendix

Annotated Outline for a Needs Assessment Report

I. Scope of the Report

As there are three phases of needs assessment activity, there could be reports for each. This outline is for an *overview* of the entire process and is adaptable to separate reports if required. The report is a comprehensive summary of the assessment but not one that contains all details, with the latter being placed in appendices to the document.

II. Front Material, Authorship, and Acknowledgments

Example Title: Assessment of Needs for (Migrant Children, Beginning Science Education Teachers, Training in Welding Engineering, Human Resource Development for Corporation XYZ, Children's Services Department)

It is valuable to identify the focus of the needs assessment in the title of the report.

Authorship: Specify the names of the members of the needs assessment committee (NAC) with their affiliations and identify the individual(s) who facilitated activities conducted under the aegis of the group.

Acknowledgments: A lot of help is usually necessary to implement a needs assessment. A short paragraph identifying the nature of the assistance and providers of same is in order. This is especially important if there were internal organization staff who provided assistance for the endeavor.

III. The Three Phases of Needs Assessment and What Was Done in Each Phase

Introduction: Brief paragraph or two specifying what kinds of need areas were investigated and what is meant by the concepts of need and needs assessment. (Refer back to Chapter 1 and use what might apply to this particular context.)

The Three-Phase Model: A simple way to do this would be to include Tables 2.1 and 2.2 here with a short paragraph or two of explanatory text.

A New Table: Develop a table that would have the three phases as the rows and that would have columns with headings such as data/information collection activities and sources of that information per phase. (See versions of tables in previous chapters.)

IV. Results for Phase I—Focusing and Using Available Data

Introduction: Briefly reiterate the purpose of Phase I—to focus the needs assessment effort and to find out what is known via information that already exists. A few sentences about the nature of NAC work, meetings held, and so forth would be helpful here.

Tables 3.1 and 3.2: These two tables capture the essence of what happened in the phase and provide, *with a paragraph or two of text*, a natural lead-in to the decisions made and Phase II and III efforts if such were pursued.

V. Results for Phase II—Collection of More Needs Assessment Data

Introduction: Employ the same type of idea as for Phase II.

Table 5.3 and Figure 5.3: Table 5.3 is a good way of showing what the data from Phase II have produced and where they agree and where they don't. Figure 5.3 provides the rank ordering of priority needs and is, of course, of major importance. *Follow these entries with a short but focused discussion of the options for further actions as explained near the end of the chapter dealing with Phase II. They provide a natural point for entering Phase III.*

VI. Results for Phase III—Developing Action Plans and Evaluating the Needs Assessment Endeavor

Introduction: See above.

Table 6.2, Benchmarking Results, and Figure 6.7: Tables and figures are good summarizing devices. The benchmarking results in Table 6.2 will have to be described in terms of what was done and what the *highlights* of the findings from them were. Given the top few needs, explain the *development of the success map(s) and show the one(s) being proposed to the organization.* Figure 6.7 contains a few selected and dated tables from the needs assessment process that would be useful for communicating with others. They are examples of what could be presented, and the choice of what to include is dependent on the local situation and what was done in this specific investigation.

Evaluation of the Needs Assessment: Summarize the evaluation, but briefly. The summary could also be a separate section and serve as the ending of the report.

VII. Appendices

Appendices would depict the details of various activities, show other dated tables, and contain descriptions of other materials and activities as appropriate.

Glossary

Asset/Capacity Building Assessment: Assessment for asset/capacity building is based on a different premise than traditional needs assessment. The goal is to determine what the assets (human, programmatic, fiscal, facilities, etc.) of the community or organization are and to see how such strengths can be built upon and enhanced. Traditional needs assessment begins with identifying and prioritizing discrepancies, gaps, or deficits. Hence it may appear to dwell on weaknesses or be a more negative starting point.

Benchmarking: Comparing performance and strategies for achieving goals and/or resolving needs of one organization to that of an exemplary one.

Between Methods Needs Assessment: An approach that employs multiple methods for the assessment and/or different ones for different respondent groups in an assessment.

Causal Analysis: Examining needs in terms of their potential causes particularly in regard to identifying those that can be changed by the organization and those that are not under its aegis. Causal analysis could also be applied to solution strategies to see how they might fail.

Cause Consequence Analysis: Potential causes are studied by listing each need in a table followed by causes, their consequences, and the likelihood or probability of the occurrence of the cause.

Collaborative/Cooperative Needs Assessments: Needs assessments jointly conducted by two or more organizations to ascertain and seek ways to resolve needs of mutual interest.

Counterfactual State: An estimate of what a current situation or state might look like if no action were taken. For example, muscle strains and sprains could be treated, but most would heal of their own accord without treatment. Or if gas prices were to keep rising, would not a portion of the population be able to find alternative transportation modes or ways to do their work without some kind of intervention?

Current Need: A discrepancy between current and desired statuses with the desired condition being anchored more in the present time or immediate near-term (3 years or less) future. (Also see Future Needs.)

Current Status: The "what is" state—that is, the level of achievement or attainment for a specific area of need. Indicators of current status can be obtained from records, unobtrusive measures, perceptions determined from survey responses, and so forth.

Data Reduction/Source Integration: The concept here is similar to what is encountered in quantitative courses where reams of data are reduced into summary statistics and indicators. The added meaning in needs assessment is that data from multiple sources (groups and methods) have to be reduced and synthesized into meaningful information for making decisions.

Desired Status: The "what should be" state—that is, a desired end state or standard for a specific area of need. Indicators of it come from norms, research, and perceptions. (If obtained from perceptions, the wording of questions—*ought to be, should be, is required, is desired*—will affect the determination of the "what should be" state.)

Discrepancy Analysis: The process of determining the difference between the current and desired status, usually resulting in a numerical index of need (needs index).

Double-Scaled Items: A format in needs assessment surveys that uses two scales—one for current status and one for desired status. (Most often 5-point Likert-type scales are employed.)

Epidemiology: The study of human phenomena (particularly, but not limited to, diseases) by comparing the current situation (the prevalence of the disease or the number afflicted at the present time) to the incidence or the number likely to be afflicted at some specified time in the future. Epidemiology also has provisions for ascertaining the cause of a disease.

Evaluation of the Needs Assessment Process: Procedures to document and archive what has taken place during all aspects of needs assessment in order to look at how well the entire process worked and ensure that evaluative input is obtained from the needs assessment committee and others involved in the process.

External Needs: See Mega Needs.

Facilitator of the Needs Assessment Process: An individual or group of individuals that leads and coordinates all activities of the needs assessment committee. In most cases, leadership will be external to the organization in Phases I and II of the assessment but may shift during Phase III to internal facilitation. It is helpful if facilitators have experience with needs assessment processes and methods.

Fault Tree Analysis: A procedure used for examining what might be causing a need or what might be likely sources of failure in a solution strategy for a high-priority need. It consists of constructing a tree-like diagram with an undesirable event (UE) or need as the top of the tree with possible causal pathways (under the UE) that could make the UE occur. The tree is viewed as a qualitative fault tree. (See Quantitative Fault Tree.)

Feasibility Criteria: Criteria used in needs assessment to determine which needs are potentially most easily attended to or resolved. Feasibility criteria (Sork, 1998) include costs; commitment of the organization; and the likelihood that an adult education intervention will have an impact on the area of need. (See Importance Criteria.)

Fishbone Analysis (Fishbone Diagram): Fishboning is a causal analysis procedure that utilizes a fishbone diagram in which the head of the fish is a problem or an undesirable occurrence with a spine extending to the left of the head. Bones coming off the spine are categories such as personnel, materials, and processes, and then coming off these bones are smaller ones—factors that could affect the category and lead to the problem in the head of the fish. Another version of a fishbone diagram (a process diagram) can be developed to identify failures in processes. In fishboning there are mechanisms for choosing the most likely ways that failure would occur.

Force Field Analysis (FFA): A procedure that requires identifying forces for and against a particular course of action and then comparing their relative strengths. FFA is particularly useful in Phase III of needs assessment.

Future Needs: Needs whose foci are from 3 to more years into the future. Generally speaking, it is more difficult to get organizations to attend to such needs.

Goal Attainment Scaling (GAS): A mechanism for placing disparate entities on a common metric. For example, achievement for a math goal might be given a score of 3 on a 5-point scale whereas achievement for a social studies goal might be given a 4 on the same 5-point scale. The values are judgments of the extent to which each goal was achieved. The *actual* amount of achievement for the content of each goal could be highly variable. (See Chapter 5 for more discussion of GAS.)

House of Quality (HOQ): A diagram in the form of a house that is a summary of the main aspects of the quality function deployment procedure for identifying design features with the greatest likelihood of resolving a set of needs.

Importance Criteria: Importance criteria are used in priority setting to determine which needs should be given consideration for attention by an organization. Common indicators of importance (Sork, 1998) are the number of individuals having the need or the problem, the size of the discrepancy, the degree to which the need fits with organizational mission, and others. (See Feasibility Criteria.)

Incidence: An estimate of the number of individuals who may develop a condition or a need in the future as in contracting a disease (spread of disease) or as another example those who might become prone to dropping out of school as a result of graduation standards being raised.

Incremental (Slight) Need: A need that requires minimal or small amounts of action to resolve. (Also see Severe [Major] Need.)

Informal Needs: Needs arising from the perceptions of a group through discussions and interactions, but needs that have not been directly studied and determined.

Internal Needs: See Macro Needs.

Key Informant: A person in an organization or a group who has a good sense for what others in it believe or think about an issue or a set of issues. The person might be an official leader or one who informally influences decisions. In needs assessment one technique might be to interview such individuals.

Level 1 Needs: Discrepancies between current and desired status for individuals who would be the direct recipients of services designed to alleviate the discrepancies. (Sometimes referred to as recipients' needs or primary needs.)

Level 2 Needs: Discrepancies between current and desired status for individuals or groups who deliver services or implement programs designed to alleviate Level 1 needs. (Sometimes referred to as implementers', treatment, or secondary needs.)

Level 3 Needs: Discrepancies between current and desired status for the organization (materials, facilities, support services, etc.). By determining Level 3 needs the organization gains an understanding of what should be provided to service deliverers (Level 2) to assist them in implementing programs to alleviate Level 1 needs.

Macro Needs: Needs or gaps in organizational products and outputs. These would include how well trained graduates of an educational system are, the skills and competencies they have, their ability to keep learning on the job, and so forth. (See Internal Needs.)

Maintenance Needs: Discrepancies or gaps that arise from not staying in shape, not using basic skills, or not changing car oil at regular intervals or from disuse of a skill or letting a system fall into disrepair. Such needs are especially critical in health, mechanical systems, home upkeep, and so on.

Marketing Research: A process similar to needs assessment that ascertains the needs or wants (as is often the case) of a particular target group or seeks to create a need for a product or service. Marketing research might be used to determine the styling, design, or appeal features for a product or process that relates to the wants of a target group. The wants may or may not be specific needs of the group.

MAUT (Multi-Attribute Utility Theory): A procedure designed to compare alternative solutions for a need. It requires a group to look at each solution in terms of the probability that it will be able to satisfy weighted criteria. The probability of the solution meeting criteria is multiplied by the weights of the criteria, and the resulting products are summed into an overall (utility) score. A solution with a higher sum would be favored over others.

Means-Difference Analysis: A needs assessment data analysis procedure that utilizes an estimate of effect size defined as the difference between the overall mean of items for the desired status and the overall mean of items for the current status of an area of interest. This estimate or standard is then compared to the difference between the desired and current status of each individual item within the interest area. If the difference exceeds the standard, it is considered to represent a need.

Mega Needs: Needs of the society at large such as national economic competitiveness, a healthy population, individuals who are well trained and self-sufficient, and so forth. In one schema of needs assessment (Kaufman, 1992), organizations would look at mega needs and move sequentially to macro and micro needs and their relationship to the higher, societal level. (See External Needs.)

Micro Needs: Needs or gaps relating to inputs or resources and the processes or procedures required to resolve a problem. (See Quasi-needs.)

Mixed Methods Needs Assessment: See Between Methods Needs Assessment.

Multi-Level "What Should Be" States: Stating "what should be" states with alternative endpoints such as ideal, expected, and/or minimal levels. It is argued that by so doing, needs assessment committee groups are challenged to think more deeply about needs.

Multiple Constituencies: Different groups that have a stake in the outcomes of a needs assessment in terms of making decisions about needs, delivering services, or receiving services.

Multiple Methods Needs Assessment: See Between Methods Needs Assessment.

Need: A measurable discrepancy between the current and desired status for an entity. (There are many ways to determine current status and many versions of desired—*ought to be, expected, likely, required, normative, accepted standards*, etc.—status.)

Needs Analysis: A process of analyzing needs once they have been assessed to determine causal factors and potential solution strategies and then to select the most likely solution strategy for implementation. Needs analysis has been misinterpreted to be needs assessment, but it is impossible to analyze an entity that has not yet been identified (Rodriguez, 1988). Some needs assessment approaches imbed needs analysis into their overall schema.

Needs Assessment: The process of determining, analyzing, and prioritizing needs and, in turn, identifying and implementing needs-based solution strategies to resolve high-priority needs.

Needs Assessment Committee (NAC): The group that oversees the conduct of all aspects of a needs assessment from Phase I to Phase III including the development of plans for resolving needs. (The NAC may be involved in the implementation of procedures and solution strategies.)

Needs Assessor(s): The person or group charged with providing leadership for planning and implementing a needs assessment. Leadership includes guiding the needs assessment committee in deliberations about the focus and nature of the process, designing instruments, conducting data collection activities, analyzing data, helping to set priorities, and so forth.

Needs-Based Priority Setting: Numerous procedures employed to select needs of highest priority from a longer list of needs. A number of these procedures require the specification of criteria for prioritization.

Needs Index: The numerical discrepancy between current and desired status for an area of need.

Needs Sensing: In contrast to needs assessment, needs sensing will not directly deal with discrepancies. Rather it is a procedure in which knowledgeable persons (key informants, individuals with special expertise, etc.) are queried as to their perceptions of problems or potential need areas. The querying may be through surveys or interviews.

Pattern Matching: A needs assessment adaptation of a procedure used in concept mapping. The procedure consists of a ladder-like figure in which the levels of desired status for goals or need areas would constitute one side of the ladder and the current status the other. The two sides would be connected by "rungs."

Phase I (Preassessment): The initial phase in needs assessment, which consists of numerous steps to focus the assessment and to collect existing data about what is already known about the area of interest (leads to decisions about Phases II and III of the process).

Phase II (Assessment): Second phase of needs assessment, which consists of steps to formally collect, analyze, interpret, and prioritize needs assessment data. This phase, which may include a causal analysis of Level 1, 2, and 3 needs, sets the stage for Phase III of the needs assessment process.

Phase III (Postassessment): Third phase of needs assessment, which consists of numerous steps primarily designed to select solution strategies for high-priority needs and to develop action plans for the implementation of the best solution strategy or strategies.

Preference Items: See Single Scale Items.

Present Needs: Needs that generally can be attended to in a relatively short period of time, 3 years or preferably less.

Prevalence: Prevalence is the number of individuals who have a problem, a condition, or a need at a current point in time. They may have an illness, they may not be passing graduation tests, they may be incarcerated, and so forth.

Priority Screen: An ordered criterion used in the process of determining needs-based priorities. A set of criteria would be placed in rank order, and each need would initially be examined in terms of the highest-ranked criterion or screen. Only those needs that pass that criterion would continue in the prioritizing process to the next highest-ranked criterion (screen) and so forth.

Proportional Reduction in Error (PRE): An approach to analyzing responses from double-scaled needs assessment items based on 5-point scales ranging from 1 to 5 (highest "what should be" status = 5 to lowest = 1; highest current status = 5 to lowest = 1). A two-dimensional matrix is created for each survey question. Results for each question are compared to the anchor cell with the highest *what should be* status and the lowest *current* one. Results that differ from the anchor cell are not needs while those closer to it are. Each cell in the matrix also has an assigned weight, and the value of a PRE statistic is calculated using the weights and the pattern of actual responses for each item. The statistic goes from negative infinity through zero to +1.00. Higher values and those closer to a +1.00 indicate that an item is a higher need.

Quality Function Deployment: A procedure primarily employed in business and industry for developing products that satisfy the needs of consumers or customers. It entails identification and prioritization of needs; specification of design features that could impact needs; estimation of the impact of design features on each other; benchmarking against other organizations; and numerous other dimensions. The result of a QFD process is a House of Quality (HOQ) diagram that identifies design features with the greatest potential for resolving needs.

Quantitative Fault Tree: As noted under Fault Tree Analysis, a qualitative fault tree is used to identify possible causes of an undesirable event. Via Boolean algebra the tree can be quantified to show which causal pathways are most likely (probable) to cause the undesirable event.

Quasi-Needs: See Micro Needs.

Rates-Under-Treatment (RUT): In rates-under-treatment, the number and nature of those currently receiving mental health or health care from an agency or a clinic would be compared to another similar part of a city or an area that does have such services. The premise is that the rates could generalize to another area if the population characteristics are similar. Note that the data are already available without much if any additional cost associated with data collection.

Retrospective Needs: Essentially, as the name suggests, a retrospective need is one that is determined after a project or program has begun to see if it is reaching the intended target population.

Risk: The degree to which the problem represented by a need poses a threat or a danger and/or a problem that will escalate over time and the degree to which the needs assessment committee judges this situation to be a concern if it is unresolved.

Risk Assessment: The process of determining the amount of risk associated with a need. Risk could be established in a quantitative or qualitative manner.

Sequential Purchase of Information: In the needs assessment context, sequential purchase of information (Wholey, 1995) could be thought of in two ways. The more common one would be that for a certain amount of budget the needs assessment committee could do a limited number of procedures and for more dollars it could gather more in-depth data (e.g., increasing sample size) or additional procedures would be added to the methodology. The second variation would be that, given what was found in Phase I, the organization would have to budget a subsequent amount of dollars to get adequate Phase II information.

Severe (Major) Need: A need of serious importance or one that will require that sizable actions be taken and/or extensive resources be committed to resolve the problem.

Simple Multi-Attribute Rating Technique (SMART): SMART is a simplified form of MAUT (Multi-Attribute Utility Theory). Values for key criteria, which are determined by consensus in MAUT, are now supplied to the decision-making group by the individuals leading the SMART process. The decision-making group would still determine the probability of each solution satisfying each of the key criteria.

Single-Scale Items: Items that require respondents to rate items in terms of a single Likert-type scale. Usually the rating deals with the importance of the item. In needs assessment, single-scale items may be referred to as "preference" items.

Strategic Planning: A needs-based process where an organization looks at its strengths, weaknesses, opportunities, and threats in regard to how it might deal with a need or set of needs. Given the four components just specified, sometimes the term *SWOT analysis* is applied to the strategic planning process.

SWOT Analysis: See Strategic Planning.

Technology Pull: Technology pull can be thought of in terms of a new technology being developed without there being any particular need or use for it. As individuals and groups become aware of what the new process, procedure, or device can do, they after the fact create needs to which it can be applied. In other words the technology pulls, inspires, or makes the way for the need to emerge.

Tree Diagrams: There are three forms of tree diagrams utilized in needs assessment work. One is a visual way of depicting statistical data for lay audiences so that they are more understandable than a summary index such as a correlation coefficient. The other forms are a picture of major themes that arise during the early part of a QFD process and the tree used in fault tree analysis.

Want: A want is a discrepancy in which the "what should be" state is beyond a reasonable or satisfactory level (Scriven & Roth, 1978). If a person has $1 million and feels that he or she should have $2 million, this is a want because the individual is already at a reasonable financial level. Wants are sometimes distinguished from needs in that individuals are almost always aware of wants (vacations, up-to-date fashions in clothing) whereas they may not be aware of needs (problems in periodontia or subtle, imperceptible shifts in vision).

Weighted Needs Index (WNI): An alternate procedure for arriving at a numerical index of need. The procedure is an adaptation of the PRE strategy and simply looks at only part of the "what should be" and "what is" matrix. Weights for that part of the matrix are reversed from those of PRE. The WNI (Cummings, 1985) produces values from 0 to 5 with higher values indicating higher levels of need. (Also see Proportional Reduction in Error.)

"What Is" Status: See Current Status.

"What Should Be" Status: See Desired Status.

Within-Methods Variation: An approach to assessing needs that employs variations of a single method for the assessment (multiple versions of a survey or interview tailored to the vernacular and perspective of unique constituencies).

References

Altschuld, J. W. (1996). *Is what you want what you need?* Workshop presented at the annual meeting of the American Evaluation Association, Vancouver, British Columbia, Canada.

Altschuld, J. W. (2004). Emerging dimensions of needs assessment. *Performance Improvement, 43*(1), 10–15.

Altschuld, J. W., Anderson, R., Cochrane, P., Frechtling, J., Frye, S., & Gansneder, B. (1997). *National evaluation of the Eisenhower National Clearinghouse for Mathematics and Science Education: Final technical report.* Eisenhower National Clearinghouse for Mathematics and Science Education, The Ohio State University, Columbus.

Altschuld, J. W., Cullen, C., & Witkin, B. R. (1996). A needs assessment workshop: Toward needs-based decisions. Workshop presented at the 13th Annual Evaluators' Exchange of the Ohio Program Evaluators' Group, Columbus.

Altschuld, J. W., & Eastmond, J. N., Jr. (2009). *Phase I, preassessment.* Thousand Oaks, CA: Sage.

Altschuld, J. W., & Eastmond, J. N., Jr. (2009, in press). *Needs Assessment Phase I: Getting the Process Started.* Thousand Oaks, CA: Sage.

Altschuld, J. W., Engle, M., Cullen, C., Kim, I., & Macce, B. R. (1994). The 1994 directory of evaluation training programs. In J. W. Altschuld & M. Engle (Eds.), The preparation of professional evaluators: Issues, perspectives and current status. *New Directions in Program Evaluation, 62,* 71–94. Washington, DC: Jossey-Bass.

Altschuld, J. W., & Lepicki, T. L. (2009a, in press). Needs assessment and education. In P. Peterson & E. Baker (Eds.), *The international encyclopedia of education* (3rd ed.). Oxford, UK: Elsevier.

Altschuld, J. W., & Lepicki, T. L. (2009b, in press). Needs assessment in human performance interventions. Chapter 32 in R. Watkins & D. Leigh (Eds.), *The handbook for the selection and implementation of human performance interventions.* San Francisco: Jossey-Bass.

Altschuld, J. W., & Witkin, B. R. (2000). *From needs assessment to action: Transforming needs into solution strategies.* Thousand Oaks, CA: Sage.

Archibald, G. (2004, March 28). Textbooks flunk test. *The Washington Times,* pp. A1, A6.

Bradshaw, J. (1972). The concept of social need. *New Society, 30,* 640–643.

Campbell, D. T., & Stanley, J. C. (1963). Experimental and quasi-experimental designs for research on teaching. In N. L. Gage (Ed.), *Handbook of research on teaching* (pp. 171–246). Chicago: Rand McNally & Company.

Chiasera, J. M. (2005). *Examination of the determinants of overweight and diabetes mellitus in U.S. children.* Unpublished dissertation, The Ohio State University, Columbus.

Chiasera, J. M., Taylor, C. A., Wolf, K. N., & Altschuld, J. W. (2007a). Correlates of diabetes in U.S. children from the 1999–2002 National Health and Nutrition Examination Survey. *Clinical Chemistry, 53*(6), A199.

Chiasera, J. M., Taylor, C. A., Wolf, K. N., & Altschuld, J. W. (2007b). *Correlates of diabetes in U.S. children from the 1999–2002 National Health and Nutrition Examination Survey.* Poster presentation at the annual meeting of the American Association of Clinical Chemists, San Diego, CA.

Chiasera, J. M., Taylor, C. A., Wolf, K. N., & Altschuld, J. W. (2008). *Correlates of diabetes in U.S. children from the 1999–2002 National Health and Nutrition Examination Survey.* Unpublished manuscript.

Clark, R. E. (2005, February). *Human performance technology (HPT).* Presentation at TRADOC VTC.

Cohen, B. J. (1981). *Do you really want to conduct a needs assessment?* Philadelphia: Management and Behavioral Science Center, University of Pennsylvania.

Cummings, O. W. (1985). Comparison of three algorithms for analyzing questionnaire types of needs assessment data to priorities. *Journal of Instructional Development, 8*(2), 11–16.

Davis, L. N., & McCallon, E. (1974). *Planning, conducting, and evaluating workshops.* Austin, TX: Learning Concepts.

Eastmond, J. N., Jr., Witkin, B. R., & Burnham, B. R. (1987, February). How to limit the scope of a needs assessment. In J. Buie (Ed.), *How to evaluate educational programs: A monthly guide to methods and ideas that work* (pp. 1–6). Alexandria, VA: Capitol Publications, Inc.

Engle, M., & Altschuld, J. W. (2003/2004). An update on university-based evaluation training. *The Evaluation Exchange, 9*(4), 13.

Engle, M., Altschuld, J. W., & Kim, Y.-C. (2006). 2002 survey of evaluation programs in universities: An update of the 1992 American Evaluation Association-sponsored study. *American Journal of Evaluation, 27,* 353–359.

Fuhrmans, V. (2009, January, 13). Surgeon shortage pushes hospitals to hire more temps. *The Wall Street Journal,* CCLIII (10), 1.

Gupta, K. (1999). *A practical guide to needs assessment.* San Francisco: Jossey-Bass/Pfeiffer.

Gupta, K., Sleezer, C. M., & Russ-Eft, D. F. (2007). *A practical guide to needs assessment.* San Francisco: Pfeiffer Publishing.

Hamann, M. S. (1997). *The effects of instrument design and respondent characteristics on perceived needs.* Unpublished doctoral dissertation, The Ohio State University, Columbus.

Hansen, D. J. (1991). *An empirical study of the structure of needs assessment.* Unpublished doctoral dissertation, The Ohio State University, Columbus.

Herman, J. L., Morris, L. L., & Fitz-Gibbon, C. T. (1978). *Evaluator's handbook.* Newbury Park, CA: Sage.

Herman, J. L., Morris, L. L., & Fitz-Gibbon, C. T. (1987). *Evaluator's handbook.* Newbury Park, CA: Sage.

Kaufman, R. (1972). *Educational system planning.* Englewood Cliffs, NJ: Prentice Hall.

Kaufman, R. (1987, October). A needs assessment primer. *Training and Development Journal,* pp. 78–83.

Kaufman, R. (1988). *Planning educational systems: A results-based approach.* Lancaster, PA: Technomic.

Kaufman, R. (1992). *Strategic planning plus: An organizational guide.* Thousand Oaks, CA: Sage.

Kaufman, R., Rojas, A. M., & Mayer, H. (1993). *Needs assessment: A user's guide.* Englewood Cliffs, NJ: Educational Technology Publications.

Kaufman, R., Stakenas, R. G., Wagner, J. C., & Mayer, H. (1981). Relating needs assessment, program development, implementation, and evaluation. *Journal of Instructional Development, 4*(4), 17–26.

King, K., & Jakuta, M. O. (2002). Needs assessment recommendations for practice from the field: A case study. *Adult Basic Education, 12*(3), 157–172.

Kumar, D. D., & Altschuld, J. W. (1999a). Contextual variables in a technology-based teacher education project. *Journal of Technology and Teacher Education, 7*(1), 75–81.

Kumar, D. D., & Altschuld, J. W. (1999b). Evaluation of an interactive media in science education. *Journal of Science Education and Technology, 8*(1), 55–65.

Lee, Y.-F. (2005). *Effects of multiple groups' involvement on identifying and interpreting perceived needs.* Unpublished doctoral dissertation, The Ohio State University, Columbus.

Lee, Y.-F., Altschuld, J. W., & White, J. L. (2007a). Effects of the participation of multiple stakeholders in identifying and interpreting perceived needs. *Evaluation and Program Planning, 30*(1), 1–9.

Lee, Y.-F., Altschuld, J. W., & White, J. L. (2007b). Problems in needs assessment data: Discrepancy analysis. *Evaluation and Program Planning, 30*(3), 258–266.

Lewis, M. V. (2006, October 9). *Needs sensing seminar.* Center on Education and Training for Employment, College of Education and Human Ecology, The Ohio State University, Columbus.

Malmsheimer, R. W., & Germain, R. H. (2002). Needs assessment surveys: Do they predict attendance at continuing education workshops? *Journal of Extension, 40*(4). Retrieved April 14, 2009, from http://www.joe.org/joe/2002august/a4.php

Maslow, A. (1970). *Motivation and personality* (2nd ed.). New York: Harper & Row.

Mathison, S. (Ed.). (2004). Pareto/Pareto principle. *Encyclopedia of evaluation* (p. 289). Thousand Oaks, CA: Sage.

McGriff, S. (2003). *ISD knowledge base/analysis: Needs assessment.* Retrieved November 30, 2007, from http://www.personal.psu.edu/faculty/s/j/sjm256/portfolio/kbase/IDD/analysis.html

McKillip, J. (1987). *Needs analysis: Tools for the human services and education.* Newbury Park, CA: Sage.

NHANES (National Health and Nutrition Examination Survey). (2004). Hyattsville, MD: U.S. Department of Health and Human Services, Centers for Disease Control and Prevention, National Center for Health Statistics.

Price, R. (2008, October 23). Cases of murder, suicide unlabeled. *The Columbus Dispatch,* p. A1.

Reviere, R., Berkowitz, S., Carter, C. C., & Ferguson, C. G. (1996). *Needs assessment: A creative and practical guide for social scientists.* Washington, DC: Taylor & Francis.

Ricard, R., & Brendel, J. M. (2004). *Summative lessons from formative processes of community needs assessment: A case study.* Poster presentation at the annual meeting of the American Evaluation Association, Atlanta, GA.

Rodriguez, S. R. (1988). Needs assessment and analysis: Tools for change. *Journal of Instructional Development, 11*(1), 25–28.

Scriven, M., & Roth, J. (1978). Needs assessment: Concepts and practice. In S. B. Anderson & C. D. Coles (Eds.), *Exploring purposes and dimensions* (NDPE Vol. 1, pp. 1–11). San Francisco: Jossey-Bass.

Scriven, M., & Roth, J. (1990). Needs assessment: Concepts and practice. Reprint in *Evaluation Practice, 11*(2), 135–144.

Soriano, F. I. (1995). *Conducting needs assessments: A multidisciplinary approach.* Thousand Oaks, CA: Sage.

Sork, T. J. (1998, June). *Workshop materials: Needs assessment in adult education and training.* Workshop sponsored by the continuing education division of the University of Manitoba, Winnipeg, Manitoba, Canada.

Strobbe, M. (2009, January 14). Chlamydia infections at record high in U.S. *The Columbus Dispatch,* p. A5.

Taylor, C. A., Wolf, K. N., & Chiasera, J. C. (2006). Correlates of overweight in U.S. children from NHANES 1999–2002. *Journal of the American Dietetic Association, 106,* 63.

U.S. Department of Health and Human Services, Office of Disease Prevention and Health Promotion. (2005). *Healthy People 2010: The cornerstone for prevention.* Retrieved March 2, 2006, from http://www.healthypeople.gov/Publications/

Warheit, G. J., Bell, R. A., & Schwab, J. J. (1979). *Needs assessment approaches: Concepts and methods.* Rockville, MD: National Institute of Mental Health, U. S. Department of Health, Education, and Welfare.

Watkins, R., & Guerra, I. (2002). How do you determine whether assessment or evaluation is required? *ASTD T&OD Sourcebook,* pp. 131–139.

Watkins, R., & Wedman, J. (2003). A process for aligning performance improvement resources and strategies. *Performance Improvement, 42*(9), 9–17.

Wedman, J. (2007). *The performance pyramid: Needs assessment made easy.* Columbia: University of Missouri.

Wessel, D. (2004, April 2). The future of jobs: New ones arise, wage gap widens. *The Wall Street Journal*, pp. A1, A5.

Wholey, J. S. (1995). *Evaluability assessment.* Workshop presentation for The Ohio Program Evaluators' Group, Columbus.

Wilson, D. B., Shayne, M., Lipsey, M., & Derzon, J. H. (1996, November). *Using indicators of the gap between need for service and available service capacity as the basis for needs assessment.* Paper presented at the annual meeting of the American Evaluation Association, Atlanta, GA.

Witkin, B. R. (1984). *Assessing needs in educational and social programs: Using information to make decisions, set priorities, and allocate resources.* San Francisco: Jossey-Bass.

Witkin, B. R. (1994). Needs assessment since 1981: The state of the practice. *Evaluation Practice, 15*(1), 17–27.

Witkin, B. R., & Altschuld, J. W. (1995). *Planning and conducting needs assessments: A practical guide.* Thousand Oaks, CA: Sage.

World Bank Institute. (2007, November 7). *Needs assessment knowledge base.* Retrieved April 14, 2009, from http://go.worldbank.org/LEH797P2R0

Index

Supporting researchers for more than 40 years

Research methods have always been at the core of SAGE's publishing program. Founder Sara Miller McCune published SAGE's first methods book, *Public Policy Evaluation*, in 1970. Soon after, she launched the *Quantitative Applications in the Social Sciences* series—affectionately known as the "little green books."

Always at the forefront of developing and supporting new approaches in methods, SAGE published early groundbreaking texts and journals in the fields of qualitative methods and evaluation.

Today, more than 40 years and two million little green books later, SAGE continues to push the boundaries with a growing list of more than 1,200 research methods books, journals, and reference works across the social, behavioral, and health sciences. Its imprints—Pine Forge Press, home of innovative textbooks in sociology, and Corwin, publisher of PreK–12 resources for teachers and administrators—broaden SAGE's range of offerings in methods. SAGE further extended its impact in 2008 when it acquired CQ Press and its best-selling and highly respected political science research methods list.

From qualitative, quantitative, and mixed methods to evaluation, SAGE is the essential resource for academics and practitioners looking for the latest methods by leading scholars.

For more information, visit **www.sagepub.com**.

CPSIA information can be obtained
at www.ICGtesting.com
Printed in the USA
FSOW02n1807290115
4866FS